BRITAIN IN OLD PHO

Telford

DAVID TRUMPER

SUTTON PUBLISHING

Sutton Publishing Limited
Phoenix Mill · Thrupp · Stroud
Gloucestershire · GL5 2BU

First published 2001

Copyright © David Trumper, 2001

British Library Cataloguing in Publication Data
A catalogue record for this book is available from the
British Library.

ISBN 0-7509-2784-4

Typeset in 10.5/13.5 Photina.
Typesetting and origination by
Sutton Publishing Limited.
Printed and bound in England by
J.H. Haynes & Co. Ltd, Sparkford.

Dedicated to the Memory of
Jack and Harriet Powell and the Rushton Family of Forge Row

The Rushton Family, Forge Row, Old Park, *c.* 1900. This family photograph shows the sons and daughters of Arthur and Pamela Rushton seated in the middle row. Back row, left to right: Joe, Arthur, Luke, Jim, Mark, Marion. Middle row: Jabez, Elizabeth, Arthur (Father), Little Joe, Pamela (Mother), John. Front row: Leonard, Harriet.

CONTENTS

Introduction   4

1.   The Five Townships   7

2.   Villages & Hamlets   23

3.   Public Houses   33

4.   People & Events   41

5.   The Old Industries   53

6.   People at Work   61

7.   Churches & Chapels   73

8.   River & Canal   83

9.   Road & Rail   91

10. Schools & Colleges   103

11. Telford New Town   109

12. The Wrekin   119

     Acknowledgements & Bibliography   126

INTRODUCTION

Naming the new town after Thomas Telford was a stroke of genius, for although he was not a Shropshire man, having been born in Scotland, he was a Salopian by adoption. He came to Shropshire in 1786 and became the Surveyor of Public Works for the county the same year. He is the 'Father of Civil Engineering', and from the very nature of his work he would have known the area well and the people in it. The influence of his work can still be seen across Shropshire and beyond.

Telford New Town dates from 1968 when the Government enlarged the area that had been designated Dawley New Town in 1963, from the south of the old London to Holyhead Road to encompass a large area to the north as well. The new area from north to south stretches almost 10 miles, while it is 3 miles across at its widest point.

Before the advent of a new town, this part of east Shropshire was dying. The industrial revolution had come and gone and left a legacy of decay. There were over 5,000 acres of derelict wasteland containing spoil heaps, pit mounds, about 2,000

Trench, *c.* 1935. In *Kelly's Directory* for 1921 this short description was given of the village. 'The Trench is a straggling hamlet about one and a half miles in length, principally in the township of Wrockwardine Wood, from which place it is nearly a mile distant, and has a station called 'Trench Crossing' on the London and North West railway. Here is a Primitive Methodist chapel built in 1866. A volunteer fire brigade was organised in 1916.' This view is looking towards Hadley; Holly Villa and Ivy Villa are on the right and the New Inn is a little further on.

uncapped pit shafts, abandoned quarries, stagnant pools and long neglected forges and furnaces; a huge task to be faced by the architects and planners.

Another problem came from the hostility of the locals from Wellington, Oakengates, Dawley, Madeley and Ironbridge who were fiercely independent, mindful of their rights and separated for years by large tracts of derelict land.

The Telford Development Corporation, given extensive powers by the New Town Act, set about their task with a passion. They did not try to destroy the individuality of the five towns and the smaller hamlets, but left them as district centres and set about linking them together with an amazing network of roads and bypasses. The gaps were then filled in by large areas of housing with schools and other amenities, industrial estates with their workshops and factories and a large town centre as a focal point, with its departmental stores, offices, civic buildings, town park and other recreational facilities.

Although mistakes have been made, the welding together of the old and new has been successful, and as prosperity grows the people of Telford can still keep the identities of their own communities alive, but also feel a great pride in being part of the new town. Telford was born out of an idea from the twentieth century, but is growing into a town for the twenty-first.

Malinslee Hall, 16 September 1962. Thomas Botfield built this house in about 1790. He was an industrialist who owned Old Park Iron Co. and various other works in the area. William Botfield later occupied the hall until his death in 1840, when it became the offices of the company and the home of the manager of the ironworks. The hall had three storeys and was built of brick; the front elevation was very grand and decorated with Ionic columns. The building was demolished in 1971 and the new town centre was erected on this site.

Church Steps, Ironbridge, *c.* 1935. A schoolboy, a milkman and an old gentleman pose for the photographer on the incline of 120 steps that lead up to St Luke's church. Much of the money for the church was provided by the Madeley Wood Company, who owned a brick works and provided the bricks for both the church and the steps. The churchyard was later extended over the steps to form a tunnel.

1

The Five Townships

The Market Square, Wellington, looking towards Church Street, *c.* 1950. The market moved to this site from the Green to the north of All Saints' church in 1244. It once included Bell Street, Duke Street and Crown Street, but these were eventually built over. On the left, with its grand entrance, is the Wrekin Hotel. In the last quarter of the nineteenth century Thomas Taylor, who also had a brewery in Wrekin Street, owned the Wrekin Hotel. In the twentieth century it became a commercial hotel, run by Mabel Chinock, and later a temperance hotel. The ground floor was gradually taken over by shops. Stead and Simpson sold shoes and were there from the start of the twentieth century. After the hotel closed the upper floors were converted into office space.

Church Street, Wellington, *c.* 1905. The man on the right is walking past the wall of the parish church. On the left is the drapers shop belonging to J.L. and E.T. Morgan, and above them are the premises of James Smith & Son, who were licensed to sell wines and spirits; it is now the Bacchus Inn. The tall building to the right is Lloyds Bank and on the corner is the ironmongers belonging to S. Corbett & Son, who were also engineers, agricultural implement makers and grinding mill manufacturers. The building in the centre is the post office. At this period it was opened on weekdays from 7 a.m. until 9 p.m. and on Sundays, Good Friday and Christmas Day from 8 to 10 a.m. for telegraph business only.

New Street, Wellington, *c.* 1950. This photograph was taken looking towards the Market Square. William Bentley was landlord of the Duke of Wellington, on the right, from 1870 until 1905. He sported a 12-inch beard and kept a rack of Broseley pipes behind the bar for the use of his customers. The inn was demolished in the 1960s and Fine Fare supermarkets developed the site. On the left is Sidoli's café, which was once an inn known as the Shakespeare. Heath's van in the centre belonged to a local baker and confectioner in New Street, who also ran a popular dance hall in an area above his shop.

Wellington, 30 June 1970. This view was taken from the top of Constitution Hill; the bus is on Victoria Street and behind is the railway station. The building under construction in Church Street is Menzies' new store, which is now W.H. Smith. The shops that disappeared from that site were Richard Brittain, a grocer and tea dealer, Bert Richards, a tobacconist and hairdresser, and Noblett's sweet shop. The large gasometer is on the site now occupied by Aldi's supermarket.

The Market Square, Wellington, *c.* 1930. This photograph was taken from Crown Street, looking up to Church Street. The shop in the timber-framed building once belonged to J.W. Owen, a clothier and hatter, and was later taken over by Walter Davies. A bike is parked outside Hilton's shoe shop and above them is Bates and Hunt, the chemist, who also had shops at Ironbridge, Much Wenlock, Hadley and Shifnal. During the 1930s Sir Oswald Mosley and his Blackshirts held a rally in the Market Square, which so annoyed the Wellingtonians that they pelted him with tomatoes and overturned his car.

New Street, Wellington, *c.* 1900. The smart carriage is blocking the road outside Arthur Bourne's shop; he was listed as a carver and gilder and his shop as a fancy repository. The lady is looking in the window of Thomas Howes' shop, which was a grocer and confectioners. On the other side of the road is Eaton & Co., the tailor and outfitter, and at the top of the street are the premises of William Jeffries, who was a curiosity and antique furniture dealer.

The Majestic Ballroom, Wellington, c. 1970. The Majestic was situated at the top of New Street and was a very popular venue, attracting groups such as Manfred Mann in the 1960s. The ballroom was opened in 1934 as the Palais de Dance by William Boffey, a local confectioner, who lived at Herbert Avenue. The Majestic closed in 1969, and before it was demolished was used as an auction room. The site is now occupied by a KwikSave supermarket. The petrol pump and house on the left belong to Brown's taxis, who were ideally situated to pick up dancers at the end of the evening.

Tan Bank, Wellington, c. 1940. It is obvious from the way the people are dressed, from the pram and from the shade over the headlight of the car, to direct the beam down on to the road, that this photograph was taken during the Second World War. The new council offices were built towards the end of the 1930s and used by the old Wellington Rural District Council. The social services and police station are to the left.

The Cattle Market, Wellington, *c.* 1910. Animals have been sold at fairs in Wellington since 1244. By 1825 cattle fairs were held on land to the north of All Saints' church, while the horse fairs were held at the top of New Street. By 1855 the sale of cattle had moved to a site south-east of the railway station where it stayed until the cattle plague of 1866. The following year a new market was opened in Bridge Street on a site now occupied by Morrison's supermarket.

The Wellington District Cottage Hospital, *c.* 1930. The hospital stands just off the Haygate Road next to the Bowering Recreation Ground. It was erected in 1912 by Mrs Bowering in memory of her husband John Crump Bowering and had accommodation for eleven patients when first opened. Local doctors were able to use the facility to treat their patients who were then nursed back to health under the watchful eye of the matron, Miss A. Bebbington. The hospital belonged to the people of Wellington and a great deal of controversy still surrounds its closure.

The Green, Oakengates, *c.* 1970. This is a view across the Green to Market Street, taken from under the railway bridge. On the left is the Coffee Palace, built in 1895. It acted as a temperance hall until 1913 and was also the centre for art and science classes until the Walker Technical College was opened in 1927. Classes took place on five nights a week, and on Saturdays courses for teachers and pupil-teachers were held. The council also used the Coffee Palace for a short time, and it was also used as an employment exchange and a register office. Duncan Ball's hardware shop is on the ground floor; he also owned the footwear shop to the left.

Market Street, Oakengates, 8 November 1966. The shop on the far left belonged to S.A. George, a gents' hairdresser, who carried out his trade at the rear of the building, while his wife sold toys, stationery, tobacco, fishing tackle and fancy goods at the front. George Orme and Son were gentlemen's outfitters, while Stanton's sold bread, rolls and a tempting variety of cakes and buns, and the Valeting Service was a dry cleaners.

Stafford Road, Oakengates, *c.* 1960. The photograph was taken from Market Street looking towards Wrockwardine Wood; the doctor's surgery is now at the bottom on the left. At the beginning of the twentieth century Davies' ladies' outfitters was a branch of the Birmingham & District Bank; it then changed to the United Counties Bank and finally to Barclays Bank in 1922. They closed this branch and moved to 38 Market Street in about 1926. During the 1930s two sisters, Ada and Emily Green, opened a confectionery shop there. Ada also had a millinery shop next door. George and William Whitefoot had a hardware store on the right from before the First World War.

Oakengates Station and the Grosvenor Cinema, Market Street, *c.* 1930. In 1857 the Coalport branch railway, which later became part of the LNWR, was able to purchase the old Shropshire canal to build its line from Hadley Junction to Coalport. It was opened to freight in 1860 and for passengers a year later. This station closed to passengers in 1952 and for goods in 1964. Other stations on the line were at Malinslee and Madeley. The cinema was opened in 1923, and was built by casual labour, the men apparently having to provide their own tools. The cinema was always a popular rendezvous, and in 1932 seats were priced at 2*d*, 3*d* and 6*d*. It closed in 1967 and was demolished in 1975 to make way for the new ring road.

Oxford Street, Oakengates, *c.* 1920. The street takes its name from the Oxford Hotel in Market Street. Samuel Lea's grocery shop is on the right-hand corner; they were also agents for W. & A. Gilbey Ltd, a wine and spirit merchant. John Dickins and his successors had a shop on the opposite corner for over 100 years. In 1891 he was described as a draper, silk mercer, milliner, outfitter, hatter and hosier. The firm moved to temporary premises at 12 Market Street, after the shop was gutted by fire during the Second World War. Halfway up on the right is the shop belonging to Harry Heath who was listed as a clothier. Note the smart display board in front of his shop.

The Recreation Ground, Oakengates, *c.* 1930. A pit mound was levelled in 1927 by the Miners' Welfare Fund and this park was laid out on the site. We are looking towards Wombridge, with the houses on Walton Avenue top right. The gates have been knocked down several times by cars but have always been replaced. A section of the Charlton Mound can be seen bottom left; part was taken away to build a bus shelter, but when the locals arrived one morning it had disappeared down a pit shaft. The mound at the rear is known locally as Gorse Bank.

High Street, Dawley, 25 April 1967. This photograph records the chaos caused by road works when the High Street was dug up to remake the road. The *Shropshire Star* headline read, 'This is Dawley High Street Today – A Hole In The Road To Beat Them All'. The County Council had set a four-week target for completion. This photograph was taken two weeks into the work and shows they were already off schedule. We are looking up the street towards the Elephant and Castle. The building jutting out on the left is Bailey's butcher's shop.

Opposite, above: The Market Hall, Dawley, *c.* 1900. Early in the nineteenth century the township of Dawley moved from around the old parish church to this area. The Market Hall was erected in 1867 and was built out of red brick with an ornamental frontage and vaults underneath. The frontage was once topped by a turret containing a bell and a clock presented by Lt Col William Kenyon Slaney who in a guide for 1882 was described as Lord of the Manor. Down Chapel Street at the rear of the hall was a potato market.

Opposite, below: High Street, Dawley, *c.* 1925. The Market Hall is on the left and the building straight ahead is the Elephant and Castle public house. On the left is Phillip's Stores, who had shops in towns all around the county. They were listed as grocers and tea dealers. The men and boys are standing outside Horace Smith's barber's shop; he later moved his business to Burton Street. The shop with the large awning belonged to Benjamin Preece and Son, a shoemaker, who traded in the High Street for over a hundred years. The gas lamp at the top of the street was lit with gas from the works in Chapel Street, built in 1857 and belonging to the Dawley Gas Co. Ltd.

The High Street, Dawley, *c.* 1950. In *Bagshaw's Directory* for 1851 the population of Dawley is given as 8,641, with Dawley Green, on which the High Street was built, being the most densely populated part of the parish. The High Street at that time contained many good houses and shops in a variety of retail trades. There were several butchers, grocers and shoemakers as well as a saddle maker, a bonnet maker, a hatter and a wheelwright. The petrol pump by the wooden building belonged to Joseph Poole's Garage.

Manor Farm Estate, Dawley, 12 January 1956. A great deal of slum clearance was seen in the Dawley area after the Second World War, as in some parts housing was in a very poor state. To bridge the gap between knocking down old houses and building new ones, buses were converted into temporary homes. Between 1950 and 1955 a number of pit mounds were cleared from this site, which was developed into a modern housing estate with 350 houses and flats.

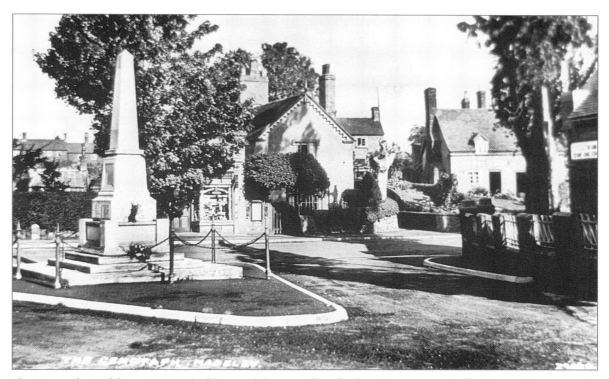

The Cenotaph, Madeley, c. 1935. The history of the town dates back to Saxon times. In the thirteenth century the manor belonged to Wenlock Abbey, who extended the town by clearing more woodland. The Cenotaph stood at this junction until 1970 when it was resited in Russell Square by the new shopping centre. It was always considered a traffic hazard, and on Armistice Day the parade would completely block the road for the duration of the service.

The Anstice Memorial Institute, Madeley, c. 1910. The Institute was built in 1869 in memory of John Anstice, an ironmaster, who had died two years earlier. It was designed by John Johnson of London in the Italianate style, cost about £3,000 and is reputed to be the first working men's club in the world. Its accommodation included a lecture hall that seated 750, a billiard room, a smoking room and a reading room and library that contained over 2,000 volumes; the library closed in 1942. During the redevelopment of the 1960s a new shopping complex was built around it and it is now used for plays, dances and social events.

Ironbridge, *c*. 1900. The town of Ironbridge takes its name from the bridge that was erected in 1779 and caused the growth of the town, perched on the steep limestone cliff overlooking the Severn Gorge. St Luke's was consecrated in 1837, and to mark the occasion James Thompson of the Lightmoor Works presented the church with a silver communion service. The new church was able to accommodate 1,062 people, and from the beginning attracted large congregations. On Census Sunday in 1851 the morning service attracted 500 adults and 80 children and at Evensong the congregation was 700. The church was designed by Thomas Smith of Madeley.

Opposite, above: Court Street, Madeley, *c*. 1925. Court Street leads directly from the High Street to Madeley Court. The photographer is looking towards the High Street with Russell Square at the bottom right. The second door on the left is the grocery shop belonging to Albert Leighton. The two men are standing outside the house occupied by William Blocksidge, a painter and plumber. On the right is the sign of the Barley Mow: this pub was owned by the Lichfield City Brewery Co. in 1901 when the manager was Edward Bowen. Its customers were mainly miners.

Opposite, below: The Old Folks Rest Room, Madeley, 2 February 1968. The building stood in Park Avenue almost opposite the Anstice Memorial Institute and was a victim of the first redevelopment of an existing area in Dawley New Town. Robert Moore, a local grocer with a strong religious and social conscience, started the rest room in 1929, with weekly meetings at the institute. These premises were erected in 1934 and were open daily, except at weekends. With the development of Madeley town centre, the old building was demolished, but not before a new rest room was built in Church Street.

The Market Place, Ironbridge, c. 1900. The Friday market was started in about 1800. The Market Hall, on the left, originally had an open, arcaded ground floor, with two upper storeys and an attic. The open ground floor had been filled in with shops by 1847. Mrs Bartlett of Marnwood House erected the red granite drinking fountain in 1862 in memory of her husband, the Revd Mr John Bartlett, the vicar of Buildwas from 1822 until 1861 and a man who took great interest in local affairs. With the recent alteration to the Market Place the memorial has been moved and hidden way above the Waterloo Street car park.

High Street, Ironbridge, c. 1900. The Municipal Buildings on the junction of High Street and Church Hill have been demolished as far down as the shops with the blinds. A number of houses on the left have suffered the same fate and a mini roundabout has taken the place of the gas lamp. The shop on the right was owned by Frank Beddoes and was purpose built as an ironmonger's shop in about 1870. As well as selling all the usual hardware he was also a blasting powder, fuse and dynamite merchant. He also had another shop in Oakengates, and the business flourished until the middle of the twentieth century. Nick Tart, the estate agent, now occupies the building. The Coalbrookdale gas lamp has been re-erected on the left in front of Nock Deighton.

2

Villages & Hamlets

The Four Turnings, Admaston, *c*. 1920. It is thought that the name of the village is derived from Edmund's Homestead. Until the middle of the twentieth century it was a quiet little village on the outskirts of Wellington, but with the advent of Telford New Town, it saw large-scale housing projects developed. The house on the left, for obvious reasons, is called The Gables, while the house on the other corner is the Manor House; both buildings still exist. At this crossroads, the road to the left leads to Bratton, Hadley lies straight ahead and Wellington is to the right.

The Elms, Bratton, *c.* 1900. Bratton is another tiny settlement that has seen a great deal of redevelopment since the 1970s. In 1905 The Elms belonged to Mrs Dorothy Bostock, perhaps one of the ladies in the photograph. In *Kelly's Directory* she was listed as a butcher and a farmer. The house is still there though greatly altered and with a lot of new housing surrounding it.

The Square, Hadley, *c.* 1905. Richard Brittain was a family grocer and provisions merchant; the shop was later a chemist's run by Bates and Hunt before it was demolished. The shop on the corner of Castle Street belonged to Robert Heenan, a grocer and baker. It was later taken over by Melias. The house in the centre of Castle Street belonged to Henry Woodfin, a boot repairer. He had a workshop in a lean-to shed at the rear of the house, where for many years Lenny Baker did the shoe and boot repairs.

The Square, Hadley, *c.* 1905. Mr Shutt, the pork butcher, advertised home-cured hams and bacon and fresh pies and sausages that were made daily. A Primitive Methodist church was erected on the corner of Gladstone Street and The Square in 1841 and was rebuilt on a grander scale in 1871. It closed in 1834 and was converted into a cinema called the Regal. It later became a garage selling tyres before it was demolished.

Beveley, *c.* 1900. Beveley was a small hamlet adjoining Ketley, partly in Wellington parish and partly in Wombridge. The small brick chapel in the centre was built by the Primitive Methodists in 1871 and was used until 1958. The path at the rear of the chapel led to Wombridge. The message on the back of this postcard reads, 'this is where I am going. It is really the next village to Ketley and joins it to Oakengates. I have marked the house I am going to. That little kiddie in white in the road is my little niece and another one just going out of sight by her.' Unfortunately the writer does not give us any names.

Opposite, above: Ketley Bank to Oakengates, 26 August 1958. This rural scene is Edith and Jack Hanley's chicken farm. The pit mound in the centre was known as High Mound and on the other side was Rag Field. Just above the trees in the foreground you can make out the main railway line between Wellington and Wolverhampton. The tall chimneys on the left belong to Blockley's Brick Works, while to the right of the chimneys is Trench Pool. To the right of the pool is the engine house at Trench Lock.

Opposite, below: St Georges, *c.* 1920. This view is looking up Stafford Street. The building on the left was the post office run for many years by Mrs Ann Edkin. She also ran a printing works from the same premises that was later taken over by Herbert Price; just above is John Owen's cycle shop. The building near the top on the right was the Elephant and Castle. It's hard to believe that this quiet junction would soon become an accident black spot (see page 94).

Stafford Street, St George's

The Post Office, Wrockwardine Wood, *c.* 1900. William Harper was sub-postmaster from the 1880s until the 1920s. In 1891 his shop was listed as a post office, money order office, savings bank and an annuity and insurance office. The post office received letters sorted at Wellington that arrived by foot each weekday morning at 8 a.m., with letters dispatched from there at 5.05 p.m. Mr Harper hired out traps and waggonettes from there, and he was also a grocer and baker. The premises later became the Beehive Bakery.

Woodhouse Crescent, Trench, *c.* 1930. After the First World War Oakengates Urban District Council brought to the attention of the Lilleshall Co. that many of their houses left a lot to be desired, and recommended that they should either be demolished or where appropriate modernised. The council also developed a number of housing estates between 1919 and 1922. At Woodhouse Crescent 185 houses were built, with other sites being developed at Freeston Avenue at Snedshill and at Walton Avenue in Wombridge.

Dawley Bank, 27 October 1966. The families that lived in these cottages had been moved out almost a year before the demolition men moved in to reduce their homes to a pile of rubble. A number of the families were rehoused close by in smart new council flats in Powis Place. Many, however, still made a pilgrimage back to their old homes on washday to hang out their washing. One resident explained to the *Shropshire Star*, 'We are not supposed to hang out our washing outside the flats. There are special drying cabinets, which are quite adequate. But when there is a nice day quite a few of us go over and use the old lines at the cottages.' The open aspect gives a good view of the Baptist church, which itself fell victim of the demolition gangs in 2000. The cottages on the right remain; one is now used as Cecil Walker's grocery shop and post office.

Holywell Lane, Little Dawley, *c.* 1930. The photographer has his back to Gravel Leasowes and is looking up the lane towards The Stocking that was probably named after Stocking Farm. These were squatters' cottages, some dating back to the 1770s on land belonging to the Earl of Craven. They were small and unsanitary with some having upper floors built over the ground floors of other properties. They were demolished in the 1970s, removing families who had occupied the houses for several generations.

The Round House, Horsehay, *c.* 1960. Until the middle of the eighteenth century Horsehay was a farmstead and a few scattered cottages. In 1754 Abraham Darby II rented some land and built a blast furnace, which was in operation the next year. By 1756 a brick works was up and running, and the Round House was erected as a pottery kiln in about 1790. It was later converted into a dwelling and was occupied almost until its demolition in about 1970. Modern amenities were poor in the cottages, and two of the residents, Mrs Davies and Mrs Hoofe who lived at the Round House, are setting off to fetch water, as none was supplied to their homes.

Woodhouse Lane, Horsehay, *c.* 1950. The name of the village is old and is believed to have originated from the Anglo-Saxon meaning a clearing in a forest where horses are kept. In 1937 there was a grocer's shop in the lane belonging to Howard Bickerton, possibly the white building on the bend, with the Hovis sign on the wall, this is now Walker's Post Office. The cottages on the right are known as Prospect Terrace, while the open space to the left has been built on and is now Foresters Close.

Double Row and Single Row, Hinkshay, c. 1960. A great deal of the area that was once Hinkshay is now in the Town Park. The buildings in this photograph were built between 1815 and 1833 on Botfield land. Double Row is on the left and consisted of forty-eight back-to-back cottages, and the end of Single Row, which consisted of twenty-one cottages, is on the right. Later another row of ten larger houses was built at a right angle from the other end of Single Row. It was known as New Row or Ladies' Row, and there was a definite distinction between it and the other two rows. In the 1851 census it was recorded that no labourers lived in New Row, only foremen and skilled workers.

St Luke's Road, Doseley, c. 1925. The village is in the ecclesiastical parish of Dawley Parva. The cottages date from about 1860 and back on to the railway; note the signal behind the second house from the left. The Church of St Luke, from which the road takes its name, was erected in 1844, but was made redundant in about 1980 and was converted into a private dwelling. Doseley Bath was a local spring where locals could draw off their water before drinking water was piped into their houses.

High Street, Coalport, *c*. 1910. William Reynolds laid out plans for Coalport in about 1793 as a port where goods could be interchanged between the River Severn and the local canal system. It was intended to become a major port to bring in all the necessary imports and to ship out all the locally made items. Warehouses were built to hold all the merchandise and new industries opened, including a soap factory, a chain and rope works and the world famous china works that was founded in 1796.

Jackfield, 29 December 1952. A lady hangs out her washing to dry on the banks of the Severn just two days before the New Year. This photograph is looking back up stream towards Ironbridge. In the background is the Church of St Mary, built from a design by Sir Arthur Blomfield in 1863 after the old church had been undermined and declared unsafe. The new church, with its unusual octagonal tower and spire, was one of the first buildings erected out of red, yellow and blue brick. It's hard to imagine from this quiet scene that eight months before the village had suffered its worst ever landslide (see page 49).

3

Public Houses

The Half Moon, Salthouse Road, Jackfield, 17 September 1959. The inn was first granted a licence in around 1802. The huge earthenware jug was made as a bet in around 1890. The landlord promised his regular customers that he would fill with beer any pot that they made. So they proceeded to make the biggest pot they could at Maws' Works. They transported the jug, capable of holding about 36 gallons, to the Half Moon on a handcart. The landlord was as good as his word and filled the pot with beer. After the regulars had emptied it, it was placed outside the front door. During the big flood of 1946 the jug was carried away by the river and broken. Some enterprising individuals found enough of the remains to re-assemble it, filling in the missing parts with concrete. When the Half Moon closed in 1984 the jug was donated to the Ironbridge Gorge Museum, who commissioned Lesley Durkin to restore it. The inn reopened in 1990 and the jug is now on display at Jackfield Tile Museum.

The Fox and Hounds, Crown Street, Wellington, 27 March 1973. In 1896 the inn was listed as an alehouse and the landlord was William Hiles. The old inn was demolished and this one was erected on the same site in 1908. The premises were de-licensed in 1971 and the owners, Wrekin Breweries, submitted a plan to knock down the inn and build shops. Buildings at the rear were demolished, but the inn survived and was converted into shops in 1975. Note the mural of the river and the swan on the first floor. The shop on the left is Mitchell's electrical shop.

The Royal Oak, High Street, Madeley, c. 1960. Madeley has strong links with Charles II and the Royal Oak refers to the tree at Boscobel where the king hid while fleeing from the Roundheads after the Battle of Worcester in 1651. The inn was first licensed in about 1831. In 1901 it belonged to the Shrewsbury and Wem Brewery & Co. It had adequate accommodation with five rooms downstairs and seven rooms upstairs, which included a large clubroom. There was also stabling at the rear for eight horses.

The Seven Stars, Ketley, *c.* 1961. Win and Dick Tart were licensees of the Seven Stars from 1956 to 1963. The inn was built in about 1576 as a posting station and was reputed to be the oldest coaching inn on the London to Holyhead Road. Behind the brick façade was a timber-framed structure with wattle and daub walls and sloping floors. The famous highwayman Dick Turpin is said to have lodged there, and many of the landlords have heard the ghostly noises of a young woman who was murdered there.

The Seven Stars, Ketley, 22 December 1964. A sad day for the people of Ketley as the bulldozer moves in and demolishes the old inn just three days before Christmas, but not before a new inn had been built and opened at the rear. It was at the old inn that John Parton founded a sick club for local miners and ironworkers. For a small weekly contribution the men were assured a weekly payment when off ill and a large lump sum for the family when they died. The modern public house is now known as the Elephant and Castle.

The Bull's Head, Wrockwardine Wood, 2 June 1983. The building, erected in the late nineteenth century, is a Grade II listed building because of its façade and interior features of Maw's glazed bricks that were installed about 1904.
In a 1901 survey it was listed as an alehouse, open seven days a week. It had five rooms downstairs and seven rooms upstairs and stabling for two horses. The house was said to be in good condition and its main custom came from the mining community. Unfortunately, since this photograph was taken the fine etched window has been smashed and replaced with plain glass.

The Lord Hill, High Street, Dawley, *c.* 1920. The inn commemorates Shropshire's most famous soldier, Lord Rowland Hill, a commander in Wellington's army who was known to his troops as 'Daddy Hill', because of the good treatment of the men under his command. The inn was first licensed in about 1818 and was registered as an alehouse, open seven days a week. In 1901 it had four rooms downstairs and five rooms upstairs and its customers were mainly ironworkers and miners.

The Sutherland Arms, Muxton, 31 December 1963. This was the last New Year's Eve that the old inn would see, as demolition was imminent. The space left was to be used as a car park for the new Sutherland Arms built at the rear. In the 1901 survey it was owned by the Duke of Sutherland and managed by Urian Cowper Pearce, who was also a farmer. On 11 October 1898 Mr Pearce was prosecuted for 'selling intoxicating liquor to drunken persons', and fined £2 plus 17s 6d costs. The inn was known locally as Smokey Joe's.

The Britannia Inn, Castle Street, Hadley, 23 May 1974. The *Shropshire Star* headline that accompanied this photograph read, 'Factory Gate Pub Faces Demolition. Road Plan Threatens Hadley Landmark'. The inn stood near one of the main entrances to the factory and had been used by the workers for generations. The landlord, Jack Owen, whose family had been licensees there for twenty years, believed that the customers did not want to lose it and that a petition was being drawn up. The inn was built by the Gardner family in 1885. It was demolished in the late 1970s to make way for the new bypass known as Britannia Way.

The Crown Inn, Woodside, 23 March 1973. The two public houses on this page, as well as the White Hart also in Ironbridge, were about to be closed by Woodside Licensing Committee. Inspector K. Collins told the committee that the police objected to the licences being renewed on the Crown and the White Hart because 'the buildings were structurally deficient and of a type and character no longer wanted in the area.' The Talbot stopped pulling pints on 4 April when its licence ran out and no one sought to renew it.

The Talbot, Wharfage, Ironbridge, 23 March 1973. The inn was licensed before 1844 and was closed on 4 April 1973. In the 1901 survey it was owned by Mrs Jane Proctor, who lived in Ironbridge, but was managed by Miss Annie Jane Toddington. Accommodation was good with five rooms downstairs and six rooms upstairs; there was also stabling for ten horses. The condition of the building was described as 'fair and clean'. On 21 March 1881 a previous landlord was taken to court and fined £2 with 12s costs for allowing drunkenness on the premises. The building has reopened as the Malthouse.

The Greyhound, Oakengates, 1 May 1973. The Greyhound stood on the junction of this crossroads on the old London to Holyhead road from about 1800. The photographer is looking towards Wellington, with Maddock's works and Oakengates town centre to the right and Ketley Bank to the left. The buildings on the junction opposite belong to the Greyhound Garage. At the beginning of the nineteenth century the inn was owned by the Union Brewery & Co. of Wellington. Its customers were mainly ironworkers and miners with some passing trade. The inn has been delicensed and is now a pizza parlour.

The Boat, Ferry Road, Jackfield, 16 January 1968. The inn takes its name from the ferryboat that used to cross the river at this point until the Memorial Bridge was opened. It was first licensed in around 1840 and has seen many floods over the years. The licensees Mr and Mrs Reg Jones watch the muddy waters of the Severn pour through the gorge; it was estimated that the waters reached over 18 ft above normal. During this flood 1,300 workers at the new Ironbridge power station were unable to get to work because of the height of the water and a 76-year-old woman had to be evacuated from her home on the Wharfage and transferred to Lady Forester Hospital until the waters subsided.

The Wrekin Brewery, Market Street, Wellington, 15 January 1975. The brewery closed in 1969, but it was another five years before it was demolished and the site redeveloped. The Wrekin Brewery was founded by Thomas Taylor in 1870. He sold it in 1901, and by 1921 it was owned by the Murphy family who also took over the twenty-one inns and nine beer houses under Wrekin control. By 1966, just three years before they closed, the number of licensed premises they controlled had grown to 201.

4

People & Events

Reading the Proclamation at Ironbridge, 21 January 1936. This is believed to be the Mayor of Much Wenlock, Alderman T.H. Thompson, proclaiming King Edward VIII at Ironbridge. He started at the Guildhall in Much Wenlock at 2.15 p.m. then visited Barrow; Broseley Town Hall; the Market Square, Ironbridge; the Anstice Hall, Madeley; Coalbrookdale and Little Wenlock. He was accompanied by the Mayoress, the Town Clerk, Mr F.W. Derry, the Mayor's Chaplain, the Revd Mr J.W. Isherwood and many aldermen and councillors. The Mayor wore his scarlet robes, chain of office and a cocked hat. The Town Clerk was in wig and gown and the Town Crier was in attendance, along with a detachment from the Shropshire Constabulary under the command of Superintendent Ridgway and Inspector Machin who carried the gold maces and ornamental staves of the borough.

The Clifton Cinema, Bridge Street, Wellington, *c.* 1980. Two cinemas opened in 1911, the Picture Pavilion in Mill Road that closed in 1927 and the Rink Picture Palace on Tan Bank, which later changed its name to the Grand, but became a bingo hall in 1975. The Town Hall Cinema opened in 1920, but was closed by 1959. The Clifton was a purpose-built cinema, which opened in 1937 and was occasionally used for stage acts. It closed in 1983, much to the disappointment of the local people who organised a protest outside the cinema on 2 April. The protest was organised by the Wellington Chamber of Commerce and among the protestors were Wrekin MP Warren Hawksley, and future MP Bruce Grocott. Note the film of the flying saucer on the right.

Opposite, above: The opening of the baths, Wellington, 26 August 1910. The pool was opened by Councillor Taylor, Chairman of the Urban District Council, and the event was marked by a variety of swimming contests and exhibitions. As well as the swimming pool the building also included slipper baths and a superintendent's house. Mr Rogers, who was superintendent from 1911 until 1944, taught the boys and men the art of swimming, while his wife taught the ladies and girls. Until around 1950 there was no filtration system and the water had to be completely changed twice a week. Prices varied with the purity of the water; 6*d* when first changed to 2*d* after several days' use when the water became rather murky! A new swimming and leisure complex was opened near to this site in 1981.

Opposite below: Willow Road, Oakengates, 4 January 1971. Firemen sift through the remains of 48 Willow Road after it had been completely ripped apart by a gas explosion that also severely damaged the two adjoining dwellings. No. 48 was the home of the Nock family and all five members who were inside at the time amazingly survived. Gas was not supplied to their home; the leak was ignited from a gas main outside. The three houses were rebuilt and at first the Nocks installed storage heaters, but when these proved inefficient they bravely had gas central heating installed instead.

Rinse Lee and the Rhythmagicians, Town Hall, Dawley, *c.* 1940. The Town Hall was built in New Street as a temperance hall in 1873, and after being taken over by Dawley Urban District Council it was used for a variety of functions including public meetings, concerts and dances. Dawley's first cinema was opened there in 1913, but it only had a short life. The band was made up of local men, Jimmy Tonks on accordion, Harry Boycott on double bass, Cyril Lee on saxophone and Phil Davies on piano.

The High Street, Dawley, 26 June 1902. Edward VII was due to be crowned on this day, but because of his ill health the coronation was postponed, although he insisted that the celebrations went ahead. This scene shows the parade returning after the church service. The crowds are making their way to the Market Hall where several hundred old people were having a free dinner. The hall had been decorated by the ladies and after the meal the old folk were entertained by the Dawley Glee Men who sang some of their popular songs. Many dinners were also sent to the sick and infirm to enjoy in their own homes.

Hadley and District Orpheus Male Voice Choir, *c.* 1930. It is believed that the choir's first president, local businessman James Patchett, was the influence behind the founding and naming of the group in 1901. From the beginning they won many prizes including the Royal Welsh National Eisteddfod twice, in 1923 and again ten years later. The bearded gentleman in the centre of the front row is Harry Jones, who led the choir from its humble beginnings.

The Dawley Philharmonic Choral Society, *c.* 1935. This choir was established in about 1930 and was in existence until the 1950s. This photograph was taken outside the Forest Glen near the Wrekin; the conductor in the middle of the front row is Bert Gregory. The man on the right in the light coat with his hand on the wall is Mr Heighway, a local comedian who also played music on a saw, spoons and a pair of bones and would entertain the audience between performances.

The Peace Carnival, Hadley, 13 September 1919. The Shropshire Peace Day was celebrated all over the county in a variety of different ways. In Shrewsbury there was a huge military parade and a civic service followed by entertainment in the Quarry. In Hadley they had their Peace Carnival, when every one dressed up and thoroughly enjoyed the day. This is the Creed family and friends, possibly outside their home, which was The Firs. John Bull on the left is Mr Creed, Britannia is Mrs Creed and the Australian on the back row is Horace Creed. Queeny is in white, just to the left of the shield and Sissy Milman is the gipsy on the front row.

Opposite, above: The Webb Memorial, High Street, Dawley, *c*. 1948. This ceremony may have been held in 1948 to celebrate the centenary of Matthew Webb's birth. He was born in Dawley and was the first man to swim the English Channel in 1875. He died on 24 July 1883 while attempting to swim the rapids at the bottom of Niagara Falls. The memorial in the form of a drinking fountain was erected on this site near the place of his birth and paid for by public subscription. It was unveiled by his brother in 1909 in front of a crowd of over 1,000 people.

Opposite, below: The Webb Memorial, 15 January 1958. The memorial was moved from the High Street in 1956 and left in pieces outside Dawley Library until it was reassembled on that site several years later. The gentleman surveying the scene is Frank Jones, who was born and bred in Dawley, and was very annoyed at the removal of the fountain from its original site and the state it was left in. The memorial was returned to the High Street in 1980 and placed close to its original site.

A landslide closes the London to Holyhead road, 23 May 1966. The landslide was caused by the partial collapse of an old bridge that took the road over the old Wellington to Coalport railway line. Three workmen, George Nock, Bill Tranter and Clifford Briggs, all from Ketley Bank, first noticed it as they walked down the bank after finishing a shift at the Lilleshall Works. They noticed a hole in the parapet and then saw that the bank had subsided, and as they directed traffic to the other side the parapet collapsed. The bridge carried water, gas and sewerage mains that had to be cut off and the road was closed. Mr R.J. Mare, the County Council Surveyor, was unable to say how long the road would be closed for, as he had to wait for various reports.

Dawley Bank, 17 January 1963. This photograph was taken during the big freeze of 1962/63. A blizzard on Boxing Day made roads in Shropshire like skating rinks as the snow froze hard and Arctic conditions took a firm hold on the county. Temperatures stayed below freezing day and night for several weeks, and during this severe winter there was a coal shortage, stocks of road salt ran out and over 500 building workers in the county were laid off.

The Jackfield Slip, 10 July 1954. The headline in the *Express and Star* for 23 April 1952 read, 'Jackfield Is Doomed, Says the County Surveyor'. The tiny village was almost cut off from the rest of the world after a disastrous landslide, which pushed part of the main road out of the village into the Severn and left many houses abandoned, some split in two, others leaning at dangerous angles and many with huge cracks in them, some over a foot wide. Experts believed that erosion by the river, the extraction of clay, mining and waste tipping on either side of the river had all played their part in the landslide. Almost two years later, as this photograph shows, residents were still worried as the landslide had not been halted and the village was becoming a ghost town.

Lawley Common, 2 August 1967. A crowd of about 100 people gathered to watch a twin-engine RAF plane take off from a field near Lawley where the aircraft had made an emergency landing the week before. An ambulance and a fire engine were standing by as the plane sped down the make-shift runway in the grass field. Then with a great roar and in a cloud of dust it was airborne and on its way back to Shawbury. The pilot of the Pioneer Transport plane was thirty-year-old Flt Lt Fred Butcher.

The war memorial, Church Street, Madeley, 3 June 1970. The memorial was moved from this very busy road junction, where it had been a road hazard for many years, to a new site near the shopping centre in Russell Square. On Armistice Day the British Legion parade would completely snarl up the traffic for the duration of the service. This was one move that was welcomed by everyone, including the British Legion.

Quarry Champions Skittle League, *c.* 1900. The team was based at the Quarry public house in Church Street, St Georges. The area has always had a strong sporting tradition. In 1918 a sports and recreation ground was opened near the church; it soon developed into the best athletics track in the county, and there were also facilities for bowls, tennis and hockey. Its football club was founded in 1877 and it still has a very successful cricket team.

Blists Hill Museum, Ironbridge, April 1985. The BBC came to Shropshire in April 1985 to film part of Charles Dickens' classic, *Oliver Twist*, as a serial to be shown on Sunday evenings that autumn. Scenes were shot at Blists Hill and Coalport on 11 April, at Jackfield Tile Works on 17 and 18 April and at locations in Shrewsbury and Lincoln. In this scene we have Ben Rodska, who played Oliver, and Eric Porter in the part of Fagin. Other stars were Lysette Anthony who took on the dual role of Agnes and Rose and Frank Middlemas who played Mr Brownlow.

The High Street, Dawley, 12 September 1980. A double boost was given to the people of Dawley when after months of disruption the new pedestrianised High Street was opened and the town's market moved back into the street after being in a car park. The grand opening was supposed to be conducted at 11 a.m. by special guest Ken Dodd, who, armed with two tickling sticks, arrived forty-five minutes late after suffering a severe case of Telford roundabout. He opened the High Street on behalf of the Diddy Men of Knotty Ash with the words, 'Good luck to all who sell in her.'

The Wrekin Bonfire, 6 June 1977. An estimated crowd of over 8,000 people braved the stormy weather to climb to the top of the Wrekin to see the bonfire lit. It was one in a long chain of 102 beacons that would link every part of Great Britain as part of the festivities to celebrate the Queen's Silver Jubilee. The Queen lit the first beacon at Windsor Castle and the Lord Lt of Shropshire, Mr John Dugdale, lit the Wrekin Beacon at 10.24 p.m. after spotting the beacon on Walton Hill. Once the Wrekin Beacon was on fire, the next beacon in the chain at Cader Bronwyn could be lit.

5

The Old Industries

The Castle Car Works, Hadley, *c*. 1910. This factory was opened in 1871 as the Castle Iron Works. In 1900 G.F. Milnes & Co. Ltd of Birkenhead had opened his Castle Car Works there, and by the following year employed over 700 workers. United Electric Car Co. Ltd bought the factory in 1905 and then leased it to the Metropolitan Amalgamated Railway Carriage and Wagon Co. Ltd who ran it until 1908. Joseph Sankey of Bilston bought the works and arrived at the factory with 100 skilled workers from the Black Country. Up until 1939 the factory specialised in vehicle wheels and bodies, but after the Second World War they expanded to build chassis, office furniture and washing machines.

The Lower Works, Coalbrookdale, *c.* 1920. This photograph was taken from Lincoln Hill looking north-west towards the Wrekin, with Jigger's Bank towards the top right. The building in the centre with the clock tower is now the Coalbrookdale Museum of Iron. The Revd Richard Warner described the valley in 1801 as 'hemmed in by high rocky banks, finely wooded', that 'would be exceedingly picturesque, were it not for the huge foundries, which, volcano like, send up volumes of smoke into the air'.

The China Works, Coalport, *c.* 1910. The original Coalport China made before the firm moved to Staffordshire in 1926 is much sought after and highly prized. The firm was started by John Rose in 1795 and was built between the river and the High Street. The Shropshire Canal once ran through the middle of the site, but it was filled in during the 1920s, though part has been reopened. The oldest part of the factory is a biscuit kiln that lies to the south of the canal; most of the other buildings date from the early part of the twentieth century.

The Furnaces, Priorslee, *c*. 1910. The furnaces were built by the mighty Lilleshall Co. in 1851. They originally smelted iron ore but were later converted to produce Bessemer steel, which they continued to produce until 1959 when they became uneconomical. The furnaces were demolished in the 1970s, but the large blowing engines, known as David and Sampson, were saved and have been re-erected at the open-air museum at Blists Hill.

The Horsehay Works, Station Road, *c*. 1900. The factory has had many owners and has been known as The Horsehay Co., Adamson Alliance, Adamson Butterley and AB Cranes. The works was bought by the Simpson Brothers in about 1886, and production was concentrated on building bridges and other heavy industry. For a short time Alley and Maclellan moved their production of the Sentinel steam wagons here before setting up a permanent home in Shrewsbury. In later years some of the world's biggest cranes were built at the factory. The works were closed in 1985 with the loss of 307 jobs.

The Woodhouse Pit, Oakengates, *c.* 1920. The pit was sunk in the second quarter of the nineteenth century and mined both ironstone and coal from two deep shafts. By the 1920s it was one of the largest mines in the area, employing about 740 men. One shaft closed in 1931 and the other in 1940. At the end of its working life it was estimated the pit had produced well over 15 million tons of coal. A nasty accident occurred in 1916 when five men were seriously injured after problems arose from the pit's winding gear. Showing great courage Justin McCarthy, a local doctor, was lowered down the shaft by sling to administer medical attention. It took over twelve hours for the rescue team to release all the trapped men.

Halesfield Pit, Madeley Wood, 14 March 1968.

Opencast mining, Princes End, Lawley, 15 September 1967. The caption in the *Shropshire Star* read, ' Once a quiet field with cattle grazing at Princes End. Now a digger rips open the ground and leaves in its path a gigantic crater. Opencast mining is the cause, the search is for coal.' This was supposed to be a short-term policy by the National Coal Board, but it went on in several areas of the new town for a number of years. Although it caused a number of problems to residences at the time, it did have its benefits. The soil was carefully stacked so that it could be replaced in the same way; the sites were landscaped and new facilities, such as golf courses, opened up.

Limestone pit, Ironbridge, *c.* 1890. This is one of the limestone pits near the top of Lincoln Hill. Limestone has been mined and quarried from this area for hundreds of years, and as early as 1647 it was recorded that three men were killed at the limekilns there. By 1795 Richard Reynolds was in control of the mines, but later ownership passed to the Madeley Wood Co. Work stopped for a short while in the nineteenth century and large-scale mining and quarrying never took place there again. The Madeley Wood Co. employed three men to work it in 1892, but by 1902 the mine was owned by John Hill who worked it with one other man until it closed in 1907. The name Lincoln Hill is thought to be derived from Limekiln Hill.

The New Yard, St Georges, *c.* 1900. The New Yard was opened in 1861, the same year as the Old Yard at Donnington Wood, which used to build boats for the company's canals, was closed down. At the start of the nineteenth century the New Yard was internationally famous for its engineering products, which included pumping engines and large gas engines. By 1904 the works consisted of pattern shops, an iron foundry, a smithy, a machine shop, fitting and erecting shops, a boiler shop and a structural engineering shop, all with overhead travelling cranes and powered by its own generating plant. By 1930, at the height of the great depression, the New Yard was losing money; no one could be found to buy the works so the decision to close was taken in 1931, with the loss of 1,000 jobs.

John Maddock & Co. Ltd, Station Hill, Oakengates, 10 June 1986. John Maddock was a farmer from West Deeping, Lincolnshire. It is believed he moved to Shropshire to farm land at Priorslee before turning his hand to industry. He opened his first factory at Stirchley in 1869, producing nails and boot protectors, but as demand grew he moved over to Oakengates where he extended his production to include malleable iron castings for the cycle and allied trades. Locally this road is known as Cob Lane and the building was once a Wesleyan chapel.

Tarslag 1923 Ltd, Stirchley, *c.* 1930. This is one of a fleet of Bedford trucks owned by Messrs H.A.L. Price & Co. Ltd of Dawley, being loaded with tar slag at the Stirchley Works. The extensive slag mounds in the area were being exploited as a source of aggregate for road building and for use by concrete manufacturers. Tarslag 1923 Ltd was one of the biggest firms in the area, employing 130 men who crushed the slag and coated it with tar and bitumen. The lorry was supplied by Vincent Greenhous of Shrewsbury.

Maw & Co., Jackfield, *c.* 1905. Jackfield has a long history as an industrial area and port. In around 1605 a wooden railway, believed to be the second in the country, brought coal from Broseley to Jackfield where it was shipped down stream in barges. There were pottery works here from the seventeenth century, and in 1883 this tile factory was opened by Maw & Co. Along with Craven-Dunnill they exported decorative tiles all over the world. Craven-Dunnill's factory is now the Jackfield Tile Museum, while part of Maw's is now a craft centre.

The Brick Works, Randlay, c. 1950. The firm was established in 1838 by the Botfield family. In 1893 the Haybridge Iron Co. leased the works to George Wilkinson who formed, with Adam Boulton, the Randlay Brick and Tile Co. The partners bought the works and about 40 acres of surrounding land in 1898 and clay was obtained from a pit on the site. By 1964 the brickworks employed 91 workers, had 3 kilns and produced 300,000 bricks a week. The works closed towards the end of the 1960s.

Station Yard, Lion Street, Oakengates, 4 March 1966. Railways played a vital role in local industry, and many firms had siding by their factories, linked to the main lines. The GWR goods yard would have been a hive of activity at the beginning of the twentieth century, but by the time this photograph was taken local industry was dying out. The large building in the centre is the GWR goods shed. The white building at the bottom of the street is the Brown Lion, while in the top left-hand corner is the Walker Technical College.

6

People at Work

The Indoor Market, Wellington, 1 August 1975. A market hall was built at the southern end of Church Street in 1680 and was dismantled in 1800. The Market Hall Co. built a town hall in Butchers Lane in 1848, which had an open butter market underneath. The company then built a large market hall on the same site in 1866, which included a large, covered potato market. A corn market was added in 1868 and remained open until the outbreak of the Second World War. Even with the opening of the new Telford Town Centre the market still flourishes and attracts shoppers from all over the county; at the time this photograph was taken there were 105 permanent stallholders. The cast iron pillars that hold up the roof have a second function as drain pipes to take away rainwater from the rooftops.

Madeley Court, 28 July 1959. The Grange, on which Madeley Court is built, belonged to Wenlock Priory, until it was suppressed by Henry VIII and all its property passed to the crown. Robert Brooke, who became Speaker of the House of Commons, bought the property four years later, and it remained in his family until 1705. The gentleman by the gate is Joseph Bennett who farmed here.

The King's Barn, Madeley, 22 November 1958. The building is known locally as Charlie's Loft, because King Charles II hid in the barn belonging to Mr Woolfe, the owner of Upper House, on 5 September 1651, while fleeing from the Roundheads after the Battle of Worcester. In 1958 the barn stood next to the Coventry Gauge & Tool Works, who used the building as a canteen for their workforce.

Ruscoe's Bakery, Finger Road, Dawley, *c.* 1920. John Ruscoe ran this bakery at the rear of his grocery shop at 24 Finger Road from about 1910 to 1925. He was ably assisted by Bob Ball, left, and Vincent Jones who also delivered the bread around the area in a special horse-drawn delivery cart. The shop was later run by John Gogerty who baked special black bread for those of his customers who liked it burnt black.

Butcher's shop, Finger Road, Dawley, *c.* 1920. This would be a health and safety inspector's worst nightmare, but the men in front of Richard Williams Family Butcher's shop seem quite content. The shop is built out of corrugated iron sheet and there is no refrigeration. On the caption it is noted that he won second prize for his meat at the Wellington, Smithfield. This establishment is listed in *Kelly's Directory* in 1922 and from the same source we note that by 1929 he had moved into Dawley High Street.

John Maddock and Co. Ltd, 25 June 1969. This photograph was taken as part of the firm's Centenary Celebrations and as publicity for a four-page advert in the *Shropshire Star*. These are the longest serving members of the firm who between them have worked 270 years for Maddock's. They are, from the left, H. Bourne, T. Mansell, J. Gregory, W. Griffiths and W. Phillips.

Johnson Brothers Pipeworks, Doseley, 9 May 1969. The Black Rock or Dhu Stone quarried from the top of the Clee Hill can also be found in Doseley. A quarry was opened in about 1817 and by 1894 the Coalbrookdale Co. were using it for road stone. In around 1920 a company belonging to Johnson Brothers acquired the site to quarry for basalt. The company opened a concrete plant there in 1926 using the basalt as aggregate. By 1961 the quarry was exhausted of basalt so the firm had to reorganise to make pipes using aggregate from their quarry at Leaton. Looking at the flooded works floor are, from the right, Eric Westwood (section manager), Tim Owen (foreman), C. McDougall (factory manager).

Opposite, below: Horsehay Works, Station Road, *c.* 1915. With the men away at the front these women took over the jobs left by the men. It was hard work as the factory kept up full production throughout the war. The service of the women was also called upon during the Second World War.

Owen's Cycle Shop, Market Street, Oakengates, *c.* 1920. Young Tommy Owen, who was just two and a half years old, sits proudly on one of his father's Imperial cycles. His father, William, had moved into a newsagents at 58 Market Street in 1901, but soon changed to selling bicycles. This photograph was taken in Ambrose Talbot's Market Street Studio as an advertising postcard for his business.

Owen's electrical shop, Market Street, Oakengates, 23 October 1981. By the 1960s the firm had changed direction again and moved into the electrical business, and William Owen was quick to see the potential of television rentals. In a 1969 advert he gave his customers 'Rentachoice', where they were able to choose from the best television sets on the market – Bush, Murphy, Philips, Echo, Ferranti, HMV, Ultra and Sobell. Prices started from 8*s* 6*d* a week, or if you preferred, they would install a meter. The advert finished in this way: 'Owen's of Oakengates. You can trust an old established firm. Established 1901.'

The Market, Oakengates, 11 December 1981. A market was established in 1826. With the arrival of the railway the reputation of the market increased and it was rebuilt in 1869. Until the Second World War the Saturday night market was extremely popular, spilling out along the main street. One local was so taken with the occasion he penned this poem, 'Oh Oakengates, Oakengates, where everyone congregates,/ On Saturday night to wet your lips, smell the lovely fish and chips,/ Beef and mutton, pork and tripe, rabbits and cheese and dates,/ If you want the hub of the universe, go to Oakengates/ I'm fond of a bit of sucking pig, especially on Saturday night/ No matter how ill you feel, it's sure to put you right/ I've tasted pig in many a land, off lovely china plates/ But there's none can beat the good old pig, that comes from Oakengates.' Oakengates had an excellent reputation as a pig market.

The Key Market, Russell Square, Madeley, 27 September 1969. Madeley's new town centre was developed in two phases; the first was finished in 1969 and the second was completed in 1971. The centre consisted of two squares with shops and supermarkets on three sides. The whole area was pedestrianised, there was ample parking and the shops were serviced from the rear. The Key Market was the first supermarket to open in Madeley and it gave the shoppers a good variety of choices. Note the prices: bananas 1s, celery 1s 3d, cucumbers 2s 4d and beetroot 9d.

Morgan's Outfitters, New Street, Wellington, *c.* 1900. L. and D. Morgan were well known as ladies and children's outfitters. This was their workroom where quite a number of women were employed, supervised by the rather formidable lady in black on the right. As well as dresses, pinafores and gowns, they also sold ladies' unshrinkable vests, cycling knickers and toilet jackets. They were also agents for C.B. and W.R. Corsets.

The China Works, Coalport, *c.* 1900. These men are the skilled painters at the Coalport China Works. Early in the nineteenth century the factory was taken over by John Rose, a man who had learned his trade at the famous Caughley pottery works. Rose was responsible for introducing one of Coalport's most famous designs, the Indian Tree pattern.

The Charlton Mound, Oakengates, *c.* 1933. The 200,000-ton pit mound was known locally as the 'Miniature Wrekin'. On 14 July 1933 fourteen students from the International Voluntary Service for Peace started work on removing the heap. The founder of the IVS was Dr Pierre Ceresole, the son of a former president of Switzerland. In just seven weeks 10,000 tons had been removed by the volunteers, with the aid of some out of work locals. The students provided all their own needs, and one man from Switzerland, who worked on the scheme throughout the winter, had returned twice from his homeland by bicycle.

The International Volunteers, Oakengates, *c.* 1933. Back row, left to right: Kenneth, -?-, Ted, Heinrich, -?-, -?-, Gwen, Heinrich, Fritz, -?-, Herbert. Middle row: -?-, Clouly, -?-, Claude, -?-, -?-, Paul. Front row: the Revd J.E. Gordon Cartlidge, -?-, Pierre, Kurt, Robert, Eric. During the work, students came from all over the world, which prompted the vicar to write, 'The gradual disappearance of the mound is pleasing to watch but the sight of men from many nations sitting together for the midday meal, laughing, joking and singing together in their leisure time is more pleasing to the eye and ear of any man who believes in the solidarity of the family of God.'

The Granville Colliery, c. 1960. The pit belonged to the Lilleshall Co. until 1947, when it was nationalised and brought up to date. The Granville was the last pit in Shropshire to mine coal, the last tub being raised on 21 May 1979. Over 500 jobs were lost and many of the redundant miners found work in the pits in the Cannock area, while the site was reclaimed and opened in 1990 as a country park.

The opening of the Kemberton pithead Baths, Madeley Wood, c. 1940. The Kemberton pit was sunk in 1864 and was about 1,200 yards north-east of the pit at Halesfield. In around 1934 it produced 110,000 tons of coal, making it one of the top three in the county. The pit was modernised in the late 1930s and this pithead bath opened, which would have been real luxury for the miners.

The Corn Mill, Leegomery, c. 1986. There was a mill on this site as early as 1258. It was powered by the water of the Ketley Brook, a tributary of the Stine. By 1842 it was driven by water and steam, but by 1912 had reverted back to water. The mill closed in 1945 and was later used as a glass factory. In September 1978 one of the kilns caught fire and the blaze wrecked the building. Here we see Richard Marsden and John Quallington, the secretary and chairman of the Shropshire Buildings Preservation Trust, assessing the damage.

The China Works, Coalport, c. 1926. Coalport China Works flourished for 130 years until it was moved to Stoke-on-Trent. Poor trading conditions and the strike of 1923 were blamed for the closure. Many artists and their families migrated to the Potteries, but many local people lost their livelihoods. This photograph marks the end of china making at Coalport. The factory was used later by Nuway, the manufacturers of rubber matting, but is now the Coalport China Museum.

Wrockwardine Wood, *c.* 1910. Harry Walter Poole occupied this shop in Middle Road from about 1898 until 1935. He was listed as a provision merchant, grocer, tea dealer, beer retailer, selling Cheshire's Pale Ales, and a butcher. This photograph shows Mr Poole outside his establishment. It was taken by H. Lord of Wolverhampton as a publicity postcard.

7

Churches & Chapels

The Wesleyan church, New Street, Wellington, *c*. 1900. The people of Wellington were greatly inspired by the preaching of John Fletcher, vicar of Madeley, who preached to the Methodists in Wellington in 1765. The chapel was built on this site to replace the old church when the congregation grew too big. The architect was William Issit, who designed its fine Italianate façade. Note the sign for Joseph Casewell's Veterinary Surgery.

St Michael's church, Madeley, *c.* 1950. The church was designed by Thomas Telford and built in 1796. It is octagonal in shape and built on the site of the old church on what is believed to be an old pre-Christian earthwork. Incorporated into the side of the church are the memorials to Sir Robert Brooke and his wife. Sir Robert was a lawyer and the Speaker of the House of Commons, during the reign of Elizabeth I. In the churchyard is the tomb of St Michael's most famous vicar, John Fletcher (1729–1785), known as the Shropshire saint. The Methodist chapel in Madeley was named after him.

The Vicarage, Madeley, 15 December 1962. The vicarage has been Grade II listed by the Department of the Environment. It was erected at the beginning of the eighteenth century and has a hipped roof with a parapet and an ornate canopy over the front door. It is unusual because of the twelve windows shown only two let in light. There are two theories for this; the first is they were blocked to avoid Window Tax in the eighteenth century, the second to stop the prying eyes of the schoolchildren from the National School across the road. Standing on the steps with his dog is the Revd Alec Lord. In 1976 the Church Commissioners sold the vicarage and it is now a private house.

St George's church, St George's, *c.* 1910. A chapel of ease was erected in Pains Lane in 1806 on land donated by the Marquess of Stafford. It was paid for by the Lilleshall Co. and from money left in the will of Isaac Hawkins. It was licensed for baptisms and burials in 1806 and marriages in 1837. The old building was poorly built so that when St Georges was made into a separate parish it was decided to build a new church on the same site. This church was designed by G.E. Street and consecrated in 1862 at a cost of £4,000.

Right: St George's church, *c.* 1929. The church has a tunnel-vaulted chancel, a four-bayed nave, a vestry and a south porch. It was built out of brick with a grey and red stone dressing. The scaffolding is being erected for the building of the new tower.

Far right: St George's church, *c.* 1935. The original idea by Street was to give the church a stone spire, but Bertram Butler, who redesigned the tower, gave it a pyramid roof instead. The tower was completed in 1929, the same year as a set of mechanically operated bells, known as a carillon, was added.

The Church of All Saints, Wellington, *c.* 1910. This church was erected in 1790 on the site of a medieval church that was damaged by the Roundheads during the Civil War. The gates to the graveyard were given by John Crump Bowring. The monumental tombstones were moved to the sides of the graveyard in 1954 so that the front of the church could be laid out as a garden. The buildings on the left were demolished to make way for the National Provincial, now the National Westminster Bank.

The Baptist chapel, King Street, Wellington, *c.* 1920. When a chapel was built on this site in 1807 King Street was known as Back Lane. This chapel was built of brick in 1828 to seat 340 and enlarged in 1897. In 1920 the congregation of this church joined with the Congregational church and this chapel closed. In 1929 the building was sold to Nora Wellings who changed it into a soft toy factory.

Christ Church, Wellington, *c.* 1930. The church was designed by Thomas Smith of Madeley and was built out of yellow brick in the Gothic style at a cost of about £3,600. It was consecrated as a chapel of ease in 1839 and was licensed to perform baptisms, funerals and marriages from 1859. The tower contains one bell officially called Great George, but known as the Gruel Bell because of its mournful sound. The house to the left is the old vicarage.

Christ Church, Wellington, *c.* 1970. Two notable vicars were the Revd Thomas Owen from 1887 until 1903 and the Revd J.P Abbey from 1913 until 1962. Owen altered the interior of the church, introduced a surplice choir and organised services on a much regular basis. He was also a powerful evangelical preacher. Abbey was thought to be strongly evangelical but steered the church closer to the Anglo-Catholic style. He became well known and much respected during his long incumbency. After his death his ashes were interred in the church and a local street was named after him. Here the gravestones in the old cemetery are being lifted so that the area can be restyled as a garden of rest.

The Wesleyan chapel, Hadley, *c.* 1930. George Jones, a Methodist local preacher, was granted a licence to worship in a former Baptist schoolroom in Hadley High Street in 1840. In 1866 a large brick chapel, designed by George Bidlake, was erected on this site. Although it had seating for 280, it was enlarged in 1890 to seat 342 and a Sunday school and other rooms were added. The chapel closed in 1981 and an information bureau now occupies part of the building.

The Wesleyan chapel, Hadley, *c.* 1930. The chapel was greatly supported by Lt Col James Patchett, the largest landowner and also one of the largest employers in the district. The organ on the right was given as a memorial to Eli Astbury, a former organist at the chapel, who died in 1902.

The Primitive Methodist chapel, Hadley, 14 July 1984. Primitive Methodism reached Hadley in about 1838. A chapel was built on the corner of Gladstone Street and The Square in 1841, but was rebuilt in a much grander style in 1879. The new chapel, which saddled the congregation with a huge debt, never thrived, and by 1910 attendances were very poor. By the 1920s the building was found to be unsafe and services were moved into the schoolroom. In 1933, with a congregation of just nine, the chapel closed and was sold. It was converted into the Regal cinema and after that closed it was transformed into a tyre depot. The building has since been demolished and houses have been built on the site.

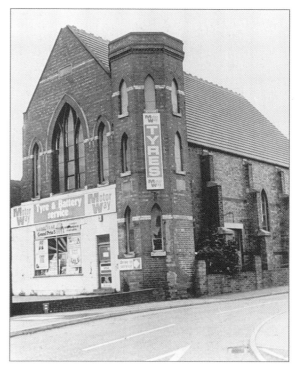

The Wesleyan chapel, Dawley, c. 1965. The chapel stood on the corner of High Street and Chapel Street on the site now occupied by the Dawley Christian Centre and the small square in front of it. The building was erected in 1860 and was a fine example of Victorian polychrome brickwork that was very fashionable at this time. Over a hundred years ago the Revd William Stephenson Bestall was superintendent and the Revd William Hambley was minister. Unfortunately, the chapel was demolished in 1977.

The Church of St Leonard, Malinslee, *c.* 1950. The church was consecrated on 10 September 1805 and was intended to become the new parish church of Dawley. However, the idea was never popular, and in 1821 when they found that an Act of Parliament would be needed, the idea was abandoned. Telford is reputed to have designed the church, which is built out of stone and consists of an octagonal nave and chancel, a square tower and Georgian windows. Dr Cranage in his book on Shropshire churches refers to it in this way, 'Such buildings are far from beautiful, but they are honest architectural expressions of what was required in a place of worship a hundred years ago.'

Holy Trinity church, Dawley, *c.* 1920. In 1883 a new stained-glass window was fitted into the east end of the church in memory of Dr Selwyn, first Episcopal Bishop of New Zealand, Bishop of Lichfield and a patron of Dawley. The rest of the building was renovated at this time and reopened on 11 June 1883 by the Bishop of Lichfield. Other guests included the Countess of Dartmouth, Lady Meyrich, Dr Thomas Webb and countless clergy from all over the diocese.

Holy Trinity church, Dawley, *c.* 1920. The church was erected in 1845 after the old one was severely undermined and was in danger of collapse. This magnificent Norman font was brought from the old church and resited in the new baptistry in 1883. It dates from the twelfth century and the zigzag pattern of more than one type is the prominent feature. It also has short, rough arcades on one side and a shell design of late Norman origin. The inner diameter of the font is 2 ft.

Malinslee chapel, 16 September 1962. The chapel stood in the grounds of Malinslee Hall that can be seen in the distance. It was sometimes known as Forest Chapel or Malinslee Abbey, but whether it had any connections with the larger monastic houses in the county is unknown. It was described by Dr Cranage as 'a building of great and in one respect almost unique interest'. In the early twentieth century the vicar of Malinslee, the Revd Edward Parry, bought the chapel and planned to have it restored, but the First World War intervened so the idea was abandoned. For many years the chapel remained as a ruin until a few years ago when the Telford Development Corporation dismantled it and put it into storage. It has since been re-erected in the Town Park.

8

River & Canal

The Coalbrookdale Co. warehouse, Ironbridge, *c.* 1890. This building was designed in the Gothic style in about 1840. It was built out of red and yellow brick and has crenellated walls, buttresses, pointed arches and a variety of other detail that makes this building unique. It was only used as a riverside warehouse for a short time, but has had other functions, including a mineral water works in the early twentieth century and a garage in the 1950s and 1960s. In the summer of 1976 the Ironbridge Gorge Museum opened it as the Museum of the Severn.

The Donnington Wood Canal, *c.* 1930. This was the first canal to be opened in Shropshire. It was built for the Duke of Gower and the Lillishall Co. between 1765 and 1767 and ran from the Donnington Wood mines to a coal wharf at Pave Lane in Edgmond. Several branches were also cut allowing coal and limestone to be easily transported. In 1788 the Donnington Wood end was linked to the Wombridge Canal, then to the Shropshire Canal in 1790 and in 1794 to the Shrewsbury Canal.

Donnington Wood Mill, *c.* 1920. The tall building was erected in 1891, although the origins of the mill date back to 1818. In that year John Boycott, John Duncombie and John Horton went into partnership and erected a steam flour mill, granary and bakery. Richard Ogle was taken into the partnership, but by 1871 John Bullock, who had started work at the mill as a young clerk, had become the sole owner. The business continued until 1943 and the building was known locally as Bullock's Mill.

The Coalport and Jackfield Bridge, 1922. Crowds of onlookers line the banks of the Severn for the opening of the new footbridge that also acted as a memorial to the servicemen from both communities who had sacrificed their lives during the First World War. The bridge replaced an old ferryboat that took people across at the same point. The county council took responsibility for it in 1979, when it was partially restored. Towards the end of the 1990s it was considered unsafe and there was considerable speculation about its future. Thankfully, in the year 2000 it was dismantled, renovated and put back *in situ* for the benefit of pedestrians for years to come.

Coalport Bridge, *c.* 1920. The first bridge was constructed entirely of wood and opened in 1780. It was known as Preen's Eddy Bridge and was designed by William Haywood and built by Robert Palmer. After it was severely damaged by the great flood of 1795 it was decided to convert it into a single span wooden bridge over three iron ribs. The bridge we know today was constructed in 1818 by John Onions. He converted it into an all iron bridge with five ribs after the centre rib of the old bridge was fractured.

Ironbridge, *c.* 1890. The Iron Bridge is the most famous bridge in Shropshire and was once considered to be one of the seven wonders of the new world. It was cast at the Coalbrookdale furnaces in 1779 and was opened on New Year's Day 1781. Credit for the design seems to be shared between Thomas Farnolls Pritchard of Shrewsbury and Abraham Darby III.

Ironbridge, 27 April 1973. This photograph shows phase two of reinforcing the bridge. After deepening the river they concreted the river bed to provide a firm foundation. They then proceeded to drive pylons into the river bed, but it was reported in the *Shropshire Star* that the contractors were finding the work difficult.

A Severn trow, Jackfield, *c.* 1880. The River Severn was the main artery of communication and trade into the county from an early date. The river was navigable for 155 miles from its mouth up to Pool Quay in Wales. Iron, coal, wool and timber were sent downstream while wines, groceries and other goods were imported. The boats used to carry the merchandise were barges and trows, the largest being the trow that could be up to 60 ft long, weigh up to 80 tons and have a tall main mast. This Severn trow, the *William Roseley*, is moored opposite the Coalport China Works. It was reputed to be the last Shropshire trow working on the river.

A coracle man, Ironbridge, *c.* 1945. The man in the boat may well be Eustace Rogers, whose family have made coracles in the gorge for several generations. These tiny craft have been made since Celtic times and were once very common on the river. They were often associated with poaching, and there were certainly a number of poachers in the Ironbridge area. Men with colourful names like Fussler Potts, Nacky Brathern and Bunkers Owen all practised the art. Speed and manoeuvrability made the coracle ideal for swift escape, and when capture seemed imminent a coracle and its contents could easily be sunk with heavy stones and retrieved at a more convenient time.

Tommy Rogers, Ironbridge, *c.* 1920. In his book, *Severn Stream*, Brian Waters describes Tom Rogers as 'a man who filled his coracle and himself to capacity, for he weighed nearly twenty stone and was possessed with a fabulous thirst. The shallower Ironbridge coracle rides better for a bit of ballast, and his great weight did not prevent Tom from winning coracle races. In the town regatta he won the coracle race, and it being a warm day he persuaded the committee to let him carry off the prize, which was a cask of beer, before prize giving. He marched off with the four-and-a-half-gallon cask on his shoulder, and drank the lot among the bushes, then taking the empty cask to the Talbot, sold it and drank the proceeds.' In his youth he was a strong swimmer and was reputed to have swum with the young Matthew Webb in the Severn.

The Hay Inclined Plane, *c.* 1900. By using the Hay Inclined Plane, canal boats could be raised and lowered between the Shropshire Canal and the basin at Coalport on the banks of the Severn. The tub boats were floated on to wheeled cradles that carried them on the iron rails. On the right at the top of the incline is the engine house. The steam engine was used to pull the cradles and boats out of the water and to help pull heavier loads up the hill. The height of the incline was 207 ft and it was possible to deliver a pair of 6-ton boats from one level to the other in three and a half minutes, compared with the four hours needed with an ordinary lock system.

The Trench Inclined Plane, *c.* 1920. This inclined plane joined two canals, the Wombridge and the Shrewsbury, opening up the coalfield of east Shropshire to the county town. It was opened in about 1794, and like the Hay Inclined Plane, allowed tub boats to transfer goods from one level to another without the need for a series of locks. The inclined plane was 223 yds long and dropped 75 ft. It closed in 1921.

The Shropshire Union Canal, Tweedale, *c.* 1895. The canal was opened in 1792 to transport minerals around the area until its closure during the First World War. The man on the left in the bowler hat is W. Richards, the last tub boat bargee; he is holding the pole to keep the boat from hitting the sides. The furnaces at the rear belonged to the Madeley Court Co. and were known locally as the Three Furnaces.

The Haynes Memorial or Free Bridge, Jackfield, *c.* 1909. The bridge was opened on 26 June 1909 at a cost of £1,600, which was raised by public subscription. It was built to avoid paying a toll at the Ironbridge or Coalport Bridge, hence the name Free Bridge. This photograph was probably taken shortly before the bridge opened, as the people on the right are queuing for the Jackfield ferry that finished operating when the new bridge opened. The ferry was known locally as Adam's Boat. Just above the queue is the timber-framed Dog and Duck public house, demolished in August 1940.

9

Road & Rail

Greenhous' Garage, Holyhead Road, *c.* 1942. Vincent Greenhous left the family business in Bishop's Castle in 1913 when he moved to Shrewsbury and set up his own motor business in Meadow Place. He was a shrewd businessman and soon his business was expanding throughout Shropshire and beyond. He acquired this garage on the old A5 from Irving Brothers. The site has been altered and redeveloped many times over the years. On 27 August 2000 the company showed its commitment to Telford by opening a state-of-the-art garage and showrooms at Trench Lock in Hadley.

The High Street, Dawley, *c.* 1973. Two officers try desperately to sort out the chaos and keep the flow of traffic moving along Dawley's busy High Street. This was a daily scene, and when two larger vehicles were passing in opposite directions the drivers were forced to mount the pavement, sending pedestrians scurrying for safety into shop doorways. The town was safely bypassed in 1976 by the Dawley Greenway and the High Street was pedestrianised in 1980.

Opposite, above: Mill Bank, Wellington, *c.* 1910. Two cars approach the junction of the A5 and the A442 on what is now an extremely busy crossroads. As more vehicles began to use the roads a traffic island was introduced, which in turn was replaced by traffic lights. The Cock and the Swan are still here, but another inn, the Anchor, was licensed in the house to the left of the Swan until 1916, when it was turned into a private house, which was later demolished to make way for a car park for the Swan Hotel.

Opposite below: Morton Coppice, Horsehay, *c.* 1900. A Horsehay resident is seen here with his donkey and cart near Morton Coppice. Transport like this would have been a familiar site around the villages and smaller towns in Shropshire, as they would often deliver necessary household items and other goods around the area. In the background is the Primitive Methodist chapel, erected in 1858 to serve the people from Horsehay Potteries, Woodhouse Lane, Stoney Hill and Coalmoor. A new road linking the Ironbridge Bypass to Heath Hill runs along the line of the old road.

The Crossroads, St Georges, 29 September 1967. The *Shropshire Star* headline read, 'Stop There's A Crisis At The Crossroads', when it reported the measures taken to improve one of Telford's notorious accident black spots. The council's attention was drawn to the new halt signs that had been erected just 4½ ft from the junction, with no advance warning and no electricity connected to illuminate the signs at night. One shopkeeper commented that cars travelling at speed were on top of the junction before they realised. Strangers involved in accidents often claimed they had not seen the halt sign.

Victoria Street, Wellington, 6 December 1968. These are the old bus shelters in Victoria Street. At the top of the street you can see the Methodist chapel in New Street. In the official Wellington Guide for the early 1950s an advert for Midland Red Buses offered a 'better way for business or pleasure tours'. For travel information you could call or ring their information office in Queen Street, and you could travel anywhere on their one-day travel tickets priced at just 5s.

The London to Holyhead Road, Oakengates, *c*. 1905: not a car in sight, just a few curious people standing in the road watching the photographer. We are looking east towards Snedshill, with the Albion Bank on the left. In the foreground cattle are grazing, in contrast to the huge Lilleshall works just half a mile up the road at Snedshill.

The Coalport Bridge, Hadley, 30 July 1966. This bridge once carried goods and passenger traffic down a branch line to Coalport until its closure by Dr Beeching in the early 1960s. On a tight bend in the road, it was the scene of many crashes and was due to be demolished shortly after this photograph was taken. Just under the bridge behind the wall and railings used to be Sankey's cricket pitch, but the site is now occupied by the new Greenhous garage and showrooms. The houses on the right are still standing.

Oakengates, 25 October 1962. This railway bridge was built by the Lilleshall Company in 1848 and has seen a great deal of traffic passing both under and over it since it was constructed. Locals either love or hate it, some thinking it is unsightly, antiquated and a disgrace to the town, while others think it should be a listed monument. The shops on the left have been demolished, but apart from that and the style of vehicles, little else has changed. The man on the horse and cart would appear to be a scrap-iron dealer.

Opposite, above: The GWR station, Oakengates, 5 April 1968. The arrival of the railway had a great influence on the development of Oakengates. The Shrewsbury to Birmingham Railway, which later became part of the GWR line, opened in 1849 with the completion of the 471 yd tunnel to the east of this station. Note the price of a visit to Wellington, just 1s 6d. A local story recalls the great rivalry between the GWR and the LMS who kept cutting each other's fares to Wellington. When the LMS brought their price down to 1d the GWR did the same and offered passengers a pint of beer at the Wellington end! The station building is now used as a dental surgery.

Opposite, below: The Portland Tunnel cement silo, Oakengates, 15 June 1968. This was the firm's first silo to be opened in Shropshire and it was a great asset to the building of the new town. It was constructed out of a steel frame that needed large concrete bases, owing to the poor load bearing nature of the ground. The frame carried the giant 51 ft high silo that was made out of ⅛ in welded steel plates and was capable of producing a full load of 250 tons of cement.

The Horsehay and Dawley station, 21 February 1962. This photograph was taken just five months before passenger traffic ended on 23 July 1962. The station had a single platform, a main building and a signal box. Since the closure of the station part of the line has been taken over by the Telford Horsehay Steam Trust. This view is looking south towards the Lightmoor Junction.

Opposite, above: Dark Lane station, Malinslee, *c.* 1965. This station stood on the Wellington to Coalport line. It left Wellington on the Stafford line for about a mile before branching off to Hadley, Oakengates, Dark Lane and Coalport. The branch was an LMS line and a passenger train was usually made up of an engine and two coaches: the train was affectionately known as the 'Dodger'. The gentleman is Mr Rushton. The houses on the right are in Dark Lane, and were built by the Botfield family in about 1830.

Opposite, below: Trench Crossing station, *c.* 1920. This line was opened by the Shropshire Union Railway in 1894. The station was on the Wellington to Stafford line, which was later run by the LMS. The stationmaster's house on the left is still there, and although the station buildings have all gone, there are still traces of the platform. The station was near to the New Inn, which was at the rear.

New Hadley halt, 11 May 1985. On a Saturday evening a number of railway enthusiasts turned out to witness the last train to stop at New Hadley halt. A halt between Wellington and Oakengates had stood near this spot since the 1930s. This new halt, built mainly of railway sleepers, was opened in 1941, at about the same time as the station at Cosford.

Opposite, above: Lilleshall Company, 1937. To celebrate the Coronation of King George VI, the men at the works decorated this Barclay locomotive that had been rebuilt by the company. The man on the engine nearest the front with a scarf and pipe is Will Lowe. Two of the other men are Sim Dawes and Ern Pessal.

Opposite, below: Doseley halt, *c.* 1950. The Coalbrookdale Co. owned about 75 per cent of the shares of the Wellington and Severn Junction Railway when it was laid from Ketley Junction to Horsehay in 1857. The line was continued to Lightmoor the following year, and by 1864 it was extended through to Coalbrookdale. There were ten sidings at Horsehay to cater for the area's industry, and new halts and sidings were opened at Lightmoor in 1907, Doseley in 1932 and Green Bank in 1934.

Coalbrookdale station, *c.* 1910. The station was situated just south of the Coalbrookdale ironworks, and at the beginning of the nineteenth century was in an extremely busy area. Trains going south from the station passed through Buildwas Junction and Farley halt to Much Wenlock. In 1905 the stationmaster was William Marshall and the goods manager was William Prue. The station closed to passenger traffic on 23 July 1962 and to freight on 6 July 1964.

Ironbridge and Broseley station, *c.* 1905. The station was on the Severn Valley line, which was called the 'Holiday Run' by the drivers because of its beautiful scenery. The train is heading towards Shrewsbury and has a GWR 0–6–0 tender engine. There was genuine sadness when the line closed on 7 September 1963, and a large crowd of railway enthusiasts gathered on the station to watch the last train depart for Shrewsbury. The driver of that last train was Hugh Bell, the fireman was Michael Medlicott and the guard was Jack Madeley, who were all from Shrewsbury.

10

Schools & Colleges

The High School, Wellington, *c*. 1935. The Girls' High School opened in temporary buildings in 1908. Eighty of them moved to this purpose-built school in 1912: it was shared with the boys, although they were strictly segregated. The school was built to accommodate 125 boys and 125 girls: the girls were in the left-hand side of the building while the boys were in the right-hand section. The hall was a shared area for assemblies and PE, but at separate times, and a large wall was built down the middle of the playground at the rear to keep the boys and girls apart. Because of overcrowding the boys moved to new premises in Golf Links Lane in 1940.

Wrekin College, Wellington, *c. 1925*. Sir John Bayley, the founder of Wrekin College, arrived in Wellington as headmaster of the Board School on Constitution Hill in 1877. In 1880 he left the Board School to found his own establishment in a rented cottage with just five boys. His first prospectus read, 'If college training is to culminate in the polished gentleman, the principal must have not only the sympathy, but the hearty support of the parents in so desirable a consummation.' Between 1880 and 1920 the school flourished under Bayley's leadership, and when he sold the school in 1920 it raised £110,000.

Wrekin College, Wellington, 17 March 1967. This photograph was taken the day before the Queen visited the school as part of her tour of Telford New Town. While at the school the head boy, David Franklin, presented her with a cricket bat for Prince Andrew. It is interesting to note the difference between the clock towers. There has been a great improvement in the food for boarders as well. In the early years of the school breakfast consisted of a thick piece of bread and butter known as 'slabs and scrape,' washed down with coffee from a tin urn, except for Sundays when there was porridge followed by a sausage or a haddock.

Wombridge National School, *c.* 1900. James Oliver paid for the erection of this school with the aid of grants from Parliament and the National Society. By 1851 the average attendance was eighty boys and fifty girls and the inspectors judged the school as efficient. In 1880 the average number of children attending the school had risen to 263. Numbers continued to grow until overcrowding and poor working conditions caused the infant department to transfer to the new council school at Hartshill in 1910. This building was condemned in 1925, but it took another eight years for the school to close and the teachers and pupils to move to the Hartshill site. The boys' classes were in the left-hand section of the building while the girls' classes were in the right-hand one. A teacher's house was in the middle of the building and in the 1920s the accommodation was occupied by Mr Tom Owen. The headmaster was Mr Arthur Corbett and the other teachers at this time were Mr Allison and a Mr Adani, who the children all thought was Italian.

Pupils from a Dawley school, *c.* 1900. There were privately run schools in Dawley from as early as the seventeenth century. Dawley Church of England (Aided) school opened in 1841 and was united with the National Society. In 1863 the average attendance was fifty-nine boys and fifty-six girls who paid between 1*d* to 4*d* a week, depending on their parents' circumstances. With the building of the new town a number of schools were built to serve the new housing estates. Typical of these was Ladygrove County Primary school, which opened as Dawley North-West in 1979. Ladygrove takes its name from an old coal mine that was sunk nearby. The school has been extended several times over the years and is now happy and flourishing.

Opposite, above: Coalbrookdale High School, *c.* 1912. The school was built under the provisions of the 1902 Education Act, and for such a small school it had a vast catchment area extending as far as Dawley, Madeley, Broseley and Much Wenlock. It was built in 1911, well above the flood plain, to educate boys and girls, but they were strictly segregated in either wing. Today it is a primary school; its most famous pupil was the author Edith Pargeter.

Opposite, below: The Walker Technical College, Hartsbridge Road, *c.* 1930. The college was named after C.C. Walker who came from Clerkenwell with his son and opened up an engineering works that was known, by 1880, as the Midland Iron Works. The college was opened in 1927 and was responsible for technical education in East Shropshire and was the centre for mine engineering in the county. In 1962 the departments for mining, engineering and science were moved to a new site between Bennett's Bank and Haybridge Road. Between 1969 and 1977 the building was used as an outpost for mature students attending Wolverhampton Teachers' College.

Poole Hill School, Dawley, *c.* 1950. The school originated as a boys' school in a room over a stable at Horsehay Farm in 1843. It moved to Pool Hill in 1846 and a girls' department was opened there three years later. Towards the end of the nineteenth century the inspectors considered the standard of education in Dawley as high, especially at Pool Hill, where visiting masters gave regular instruction in art and drawing. In 1945 it became a secondary modern school, and by 1955 it was an all age school taking senior pupils from five feeder schools. After the erection of Dawley Modern School in 1956 it became a primary school again, and ten years later, when a separate infant school was built next door, it became a junior school. On 1 August 1977 the school was gutted by fire and had to be demolished. It was never rebuilt, but the infant school next to it was developed into a primary school and renamed the Captain Webb. The buildings at the rear were erected in about 1948 to cope with extra pupils after the school leaving age had been raised.

11

Telford New Town

Telford town centre, 14 March 1972. John Dugdale, the chairman of Telford Development Corporation, pours the first skip of concrete to mark the beginning of the first phase of the building of the new town centre. The plans were for 268,750 sq ft of retail shopping space, which would include shops, a supermarket and a hypermarket. There would also be a large car park, but all on one level. One note of opposition came from the Chamber of Commerce for Dawley, Oakengates and Wellington, who were afraid that the new centre would affect their trade.

The M54 motorway, 31 July 1975. During 1972 work started on the first phase of the new M54 motorway that would eventually link the new town with the M6. The first 4½-mile section was known as the Wellington bypass, which was opened by Mr John Dugdale, the Lord Lieutenant of Shropshire, on 11 December 1975. This photograph, taken five months earlier, shows the Hollingswood end of the motorway. The bridges from the left are the Dawley to Priorslee road, the Queenswood footbridge, and the Overdale to Redlake bridge. The final phase of the motorway linking up with the M6 was opened by Nicholas Ridley, the Minister of Transport, in November 1983.

Opposite, above, Telford town centre, 12 July 1972. This view of the town centre was taken just four months after John Dugdale poured the first skip of concrete. Work progressed well; in the foreground the basement under the main shopping area is being constructed, while in the distance is the skeleton of the new 100,500 sq ft hypermarket.

Opposite, below: Sutton Hill, 18 March 1967. During her tour of Telford the Queen, watched by Sir Reginald Pearson, chairman of the Dawley Development Corporation, unveiled this plaque to mark her visit to the new housing estate. The Queen also visited the house of the estate's first residents, Mr and Mrs Geoffrey Davies. She spent ten minutes talking and looking around the house, but declined a cup of tea offered by Mrs Davies. During her tour of Telford the Queen also opened a new factory at Tweedale and visited Wrekin College.

Madeley town centre, 15 September 1971. When Dawley New Town was being planned it was decided to develop three district centres, at Dawley, Madeley and Stirchley, to give residents in the new housing estates a whole range of social, recreational and shopping facilities on their doorsteps. Mr Gerald Brook-Taylor, the Telford Development Corporation Social Relations Officer, said, 'planners had tried to build a town which gave inhabitants free movement'.

Telford town centre, 16 October 1980. One of the largest cranes in Britain lifts the new beehive dome space frame into position to crown phase two of the new town centre. This phase was thought to cost in the region of £4½ million and it was hoped to attract big name stores as well as smaller shops, selling a variety of goods.

Oakengates Town Hall, 21 April 1967. The new town hall was designed by Maurice R. Day and Associates of Henley-on-Thames and erected by local builders Pat Smith and Sons (Oakengates) Ltd. It has been the venue for many high-class performers over the years. It changed its name to the Oakengates Theatre in 1991.

The Town Hall, Oakengates, 25 May 1968. Sir Gordon Richards, the jockey, returned to the place of his birth to officially open Oakengates' new £150,000 town hall. He spoke with pride at the progress made by his old town and of the integral part the new hall would play in the development of Oakengates town centre. Unfortunately, the weather was unkind and rain forced the council to hold the opening ceremony inside the hall.

Telford Central railway station, 10 August 1985. This station was built at Hollinswood, within easy walking distance of the new town centre. With just nine months before the formal opening, the two main platforms are down, but the car park, ticket office, waiting rooms and other services have still to be erected. The two 90 ft platforms were long enough for Intercity trains.

Telford Central railway station, 12 May 1986. Lord Murray of Telford and Epping formally opened the station that was built jointly by British Rail and the Telford Development Corporation. Lord Murray was born in Hadley in 1922 and was brought up in the area. As Len Murray he was the highly respected General Secretary of the TUC for many years.

Telford Ice Rink, 18 February 1984. The main entrance to the ice rink is by the lake and beneath a distinctive overhanging canopy. It cost in the region of £2.6 million and was designed to take on other roles such as pop concerts, exhibitions and ice hockey. It was built to cater for up to 4,000 people. Princess Anne formally opened the ice rink in October 1984.

Telford Ice Rink, 24 April 1984. The structure is made of simple steel portal frames. The rink is a concrete slab holding the refrigeration tube grid suspended so as to allow warm air to circulate below. The spectator gallery is of reinforced concrete on load-bearing concrete-block walls. The colour scheme of blue and grey was chosen to reflect the activity inside.

Telford town centre, 26 November 1979. The town centre was built on the site of Malinslee Hall and Chapel (see page 82). By 1979 the first phase had created around 1,200 jobs; this was the second phase, which was hoped would create about another 1,000. The corporation also built three large office blocks near the town centre; they were Malinslee House, Walker House and Darby House.

Telford town centre, c. 1980. As well as shops and offices, it was the hope of the development corporation to add a number of recreational facilities to the centre. These were to include a multi-screen cinema, ice rink, library, theatre, racquet centre, swimming pool and sauna, art centre and nightclub, most of which have materialised. The corporation also provided over 4,000 free car parking spaces, all within easy walking distance of the town centre facilities.

Wombridge Interchange, 20 February 1980. Diversions were in operation at the busy Wombridge Interchange, while work was carried out on the 1½ mile long final stage of the Eastern Primary Road. The new road cost in the region of £7½ million and provides an uninterrupted drive from Trench to Sutton Hill. In the background is part of the Middle Pool.

Jackfield Bridge, 28 May 1994. This bridge was built to replace the old Free Bridge, which was an early example of a reinforced concrete bridge, built in 1909. By the 1990s the concrete was beginning to crumble and the bridge was becoming unsafe, and in spite of attempts to save it, the demolition men moved in and it was replaced by this modern structure. A part of the old bridge is preserved at the southern end of the new bridge.

Thomas Telford's Statue, April 1988. In 1985 sculptor André Wallace was commissioned by Telford Development Corporation for a monumental centrepiece for the town's new Civic Square. The idea approved was a slightly larger than life statue in bronze of Telford, leaning on cast-iron letters of his name and looking east as if surveying the new town centre and beyond. His coat, hanging on the final letter, looked so real that at the unveiling ceremony an agitated cameraman asked his assistant to remove it so he could start filming.

1 2

The Wrekin

The Wrekin from the Ercall, *c.* 1935. The Wrekin, which stands at 1,334 ft, is not the highest point on the Shropshire landscape, but its commanding position on the Severn Plain dominates the surrounding countryside. The hill is in the shape of a hog's back and is comprised mainly of ancient volcanic rock. This rhyme shows the pride Salopians have in this famous landmark. 'Proud Salopia's sons and daughters./ Whereso'er the flag unfurled./ Still they look upon the Wrekin./ As the centre of the world.'

The Forest Glen, *c.* 1930. The Forest Glen was built in 1889 and run by Henry Pointon. It was always a favourite meeting place for visitors and during the 1930s, catering for picnics and coach parties, motor and cycling clubs, special anniversaries, dinner parties, whist drives and dances. The Ironbridge Gorge Museum rescued it in 1990, when it was about to be demolished, and re-erected it on the Green at Blists Hill where it is now used as a Victorian tearoom.

The Forest Glen, *c.* 1930. The building was made of wood and was light and airy. It was built by Henry Pointon and was run by his family for about 100 years being passed on first to Ossie and then to Percy. The Pointons came from a family of painters and decorators; Henry had also been licensee of the Railway Hotel and Red Lion in Wellington, before opening the Forest Glen. Many organisations, such as the Masons, the Round Table and the Rotary Club, organised dinners there, and during the evening one of the toasts would be 'To All Friends Around The Wrekin'.

The Needle's Eye, *c.* 1925. The Needle's Eye is a narrow cleft in the side of the hill, which all true Salopians are supposed to pass through. Young ladies who pass through are supposed to kiss their young man on the other side or he can demand a forfeit. If the girl looks back as she passes through it is said she will never marry. The cleft also has religious connections, as it was supposed to have been formed at the precise moment that Christ died on the cross and the curtain in the temple in Jerusalem was ripped in two.

Walking up the Wrekin, *c.* 1910. Taking a Sunday stroll up the Wrekin has always been popular, but, thankfully, modern dress allows you to wear something more appropriate than the outfits these ladies are wearing on a hot summer's day. Until the middle of the nineteenth century an annual event for the working classes was the Wrekin Wake, which was held on the first Sunday in May. It attracted crowds from far and wide with its ale booths, gambling tables, gingerbread stalls, swing boats and merry-go-rounds. Traditionally the wake always ended in a pitched battle between the colliers and the yeomen for the possession of the hill. The battles were fierce and men from both sides were often badly injured. Eventually the behaviour became so disorderly that the local magistrates ordered that the Wakes should be ended.

The Wrekin Hill Climb, 23 June 1929. This fully loaded Chevrolet, 6-cylinder, 30 cwt truck was the first vehicle to climb the Wrekin. The publicity stunt was to draw attention to the Shrewsbury Motor Show staged by Vincent Greenhous at his garage and showrooms in St Julian's Friars. The truck was driven by Mr E.G. Hotchkiss, a member of the sales staff, and was carrying a net load of 1 ton 12 cwt 2 qtrs.

Opposite: The Wrekin Cottage, *c.* 1900. Although the Wakes died out, people still used the hill for social and recreational pursuits, so there was a need to cater for these people at weekends and during the summer months. Halfway up the hill was Wrekin Cottage, also known as Halfway House or Upper Cottage. Climbers could put in their order for ham and eggs, tea or mineral water on the way up and it would be ready for them on the way down. A number of children's amusements were available, including ponies and goats, donkey rides and swing-boats, known locally as swingle-boats.

The Wrekin beacon, *c.* 1960. The sight of the beacon gave travellers young and old a warm glow as they returned to Shropshire after a long trip. Men from the airfield at Atcham erected the RAF Chance Light during the Second World War. It was to stop aeroplanes from crashing into the hill in the dark and as a point of navigation. It was maintained for many years by Jim Bishop who worked as an electrician for the RAF first at High Ercall and then at Shawbury.

The Wrekin beacon, 27 August 1970. With no hope of being switched back on, one of Shropshire's most famous landmarks was finally demolished by a team of local workmen and airmen from RAF Shawbury. For years there were rumours that it had been shipped to Australia and was erected on top of Sydney Harbour Bridge, but these rumours were unfounded and the light was almost certainly scrapped. A new beacon was erected on top of the television mast to celebrate the new millennium.

Opposite, below: The Wrekin beacon, 8 April 1965. The beacon had been switched off by the RAF on the stroke of midnight on New Year's Day 1965. There was a great outcry and a committee was formed to raise money and to fight for its revival. At first the committee was successful. In this photograph we see Sqn Ldr F.T. Cooper hand over the key of the Wrekin Beacon to Mr R.G. Lawson, a member of the Wrekin Beacon Preservation Trust Executive Committee. The light was switched back on at Easter that year, but was soon turned off again through lack of financial backing.

ACKNOWLEDGEMENTS

I am indebted to Adrian Faber, the Editor of the *Shropshire Star*, for allowing me access to the *Star*'s photograph library and to Toby Neal who has written so many interesting and informative articles on Shropshire history for the paper for a number of years. I would like to thank Jim and Barbara Ball for allowing me to copy so many of their photographs and for sharing with me their vast local knowledge of the area. A very special thanks goes to the members of the Tuesday, Thursday and Friday groups at the Day Centre of the Wellington branch of the Shropshire and Mid-Wales Hospice at Portway House. Their enthusiasm for old Telford is catching; I have greatly enjoyed my visits and have learned a great deal about the area when showing them slides of the old towns and villages. I am also very grateful to the late Phyllis Drake, who entrusted me with some wonderful old photographs and glass negatives of the Ironbridge area. My thanks also goes to Kim Beresford, Lin Horler, Mrs Lister and Malcolm Peele who have all lent me photographs; and to the many parents and relations of pupils from Ladygrove C.P. School who have also loaned items from their own personal collections. I must also thank my father-in-law, Joe Powell, to whose family this book is dedicated, for the photographs and all the help and information he has given me during our conversations over the years. I would also like to acknowledge the friendly help and advice I have received from all the staff at the Shropshire Records and Research Centre. As always, a very special thanks to Robert Evans of Abbeycolor for all his help and hard work in preparing the photographs for this book.

BIBLIOGRAPHY

Baugh, G.C., ed., *The Victoria History of Shropshire*, vol XI, OUP, 1985

De Soissons, M., *Telford: The Making of Shropshire's New Town*, Swan Hill Press, 1991

Eaton, A.G., *Madeley in Old Picture Postcards*, Zaltbommel/Netherlands, 1990

Evans, G., *Lost Villages of Telford*, S.B. Publications, 1991

——, *Wellington: A Portrait in Old Photographs and Picture Postcards*, S.B. Publications

——, *Wellington in Old Picture Postcards*, Zaltbommel/Netherlands,1990

Evans, G., and Briscoe R., *Telford: A Pictorial History*, Phillimore, 1995

Gale, W.K.V. and Nicholls, C.R., *The Lilleshall Company Limited*, Moorland, 1979

Gilder, T., *Hadley in Old Picture Postcards*, Zaltbommel/Netherlands, 1998

Hayman, R. and Horton, W. *Ironbridge History and Guide*, Tempus, 1999

Powell, J. and Vanns M.A., *North Telford*, Chalford, 1995

——, *South Telford*, Chalford, 1995

Oakengates in the Words of the Oakengates People, Telford Community Arts, 1987

Raven, M., *A Shropshire Gazetteer*, M. Raven, 1989

Shropshire County Guide, Shropshire County Council, 1980 and 1989

Trinder, B., *The Darbys of Coalbrookedale*, Philmore, 1974

——, *The Industrial Archaelogy of Shropshire*, Plillimore, 1996

BRITAIN IN OLD PHOTOGRAPHS

Avon

Along the Avon

Bedfordshire

Bedfordshire at War
Leighton Buzzard &
    Linslade

Berkshire

Around Maidenhead
Forgotten Thames

Buckinghamshire

Amersham
Aylesbury in the 1960s
Aylesbury Past &
    Present
Bletchley
Bradwell Past &
    Present
Buckingham & District
Stony Stratford: A Third
    Selection

Cambridgeshire

Wisbech

Channel Islands

Jersey: A Third Selection

Cleveland

Stockton-on-Tees

Cornwall

Cornwall

Cumbria

Cumbrian Railways
Lake Counties at Work
Around Carlisle

Derbyshire

Ashbourne
Dronfield
Matlock

Devon

Bideford
Colyton & Seaton
Dartmoor

Exeter

Exeter Yesterday &
    Today
Exmouth & Budleigh
    Salterton
Newton Abbot

Dorset

Dorset Railways
Poole

Durham

Around Durham
Bishop Auckland
Durham: Cathedral City
Durham Railways
Teesdale
Teesdale: A Second
    Selection

Essex

Braintree & Bocking at
    Work
Chadwell Heath
Chelmsford Past &
    Present
Clacton-on-Sea
Essex Railways
From Ilford to
    Hainault
Maldon and the
    Blackwater
Mersea Island
Southend-on-Sea Past &
    Present

Gloucestershire

Around Bishop's Cleeve &
    Winchcombe
Around Cirencester
Charlton Kings
Cheltenham
Gloucester
Gloucestershire CCC
Leckhampton
North Gloucestershire at
    War
South Gloucestershire at
    War
Uley, Dursley & Cam

Hampshire

Fleet: A Second Selection

Herefordshire

Herefordshire Railways

Hertfordshire

Letchworth
Stevenage

Humberside

Around Grimsby
Grimsby
Holderness

Isle of Man

Manx Railways &
    Tramways
TT Races

Isle of Wight

Ventnor & District
Sandown & Shanklin

Kent

Chatham Dockyard
Chislehurst & Sidcup
Gravesend & Northfleet
Herne Bay Revisited
High Weald: A Second
    Selection
Lympne Airfield
Sittingbourne &
    Milton Regis Past &
    Present

Lancashire

Blackburn
Blackpool
Bolton
Bolton Wanderers
Chorlton-cum-Hardy
Clitheroe
Lancaster & District
    Revisited
Lytham St Annes
Macclesfield
Ormskirk & District:
    A Second Selection
Preston

Leicestershire

Leicestershire People
Leicestershire at Work
Loughborough

Market Harborough
River Soar

Lincolnshire

Boston
Grantham
Lincoln
Lincoln Cathedral
Lincolnshire Wolds
Postwar Lincoln
Skegness

London

Barnet & the Hadleys
Barnet Past & Present
Bexley
Chadwell Heath
Forgotten Thames
Hackney Past & Present
Harrow Past & Present
Around Hayes & West
    Drayton: A Second
    Selection
Lambeth 1950–70
Lewisham & Deptford:
    A Third Selection
Middlesex CCC
Queen's Park Rangers
Richmond
Richmond Past & Present
Southgate
Stoke Newington, Stamford
    Hill & Upper Clapton
Streatham: A Second
    Selection
Uxbridge People
Waltham Forest
Wandsworth, Battersea &
    Putney
Wembley & Kingsbury
Willesden

Manchester

Manchester: A Third
    Selection

Merseyside

Liverpool

Norfolk

North Walsham & District
North Walsham & District:
    A Second Selection
North Norfolk Coast

Northamptonshire

Northampton Past & Present

Nottinghamshire

Arnold & Bestwood:
  A Second Selection
Kirkby in Ashfield:
  A Second Selection
Nottinghamshire at Work
Nottingham Past & Present

Oxfordshire

Around Abingdon
Around Didcot
Around Henley-on-Thames
Around Wheatley
Around Witney
Around Woodstock
Banbury
Banbury Past & Present
Cowley & East Oxford Past
  & Present
Forgotten Thames
Garsington
Henley-on-Thames Past &
  Present
Literary Oxford
Oxford
Oxfordshire at Play
Oxfordshire at School
Wantage, Faringdon & The
  Vale Villages
Witney

Shropshire

Shropshire Railways
South Shropshire
Telford

Somerset

Chard & Ilminster

Staffordshire

Aldridge Revisited
Kinver & Enville: A Second
  Selection

Newcastle-under-Lyme Past
  & Present
Pattingham & Wombourne
Stafford
Stoke-on-Trent Past &
  Present

Suffolk

Bury St Edmunds
Lowestoft Past & Present
Southwold
Stowmarket
Suffolk Transport
Suffolk at Work: A Second
  Selection

Surrey

Cheam & Belmont
Esher
Richmond
Walton upon Thames &
  Weybridge

Sussex

Around East Grinstead
Around Heathfield:
  A Second Selection
Bishopstone & Seaford:
  A Second Selection
Eastbourne Past & Present
High Weald: A Second
  Selection
Horsham Past & Present
Lancing
Palace Pier, Brighton
RAF Tangmere
Rye & Winchelsea

Tyne & Wear

Whitley Bay

Warwickshire

Around Leamington Spa
Around Leamington Spa:
  A Second Selection
Around Bulkington
Bedworth Past & Present
Knowle & Dorridge

Nuneaton Past & Present
Rugby: A Second Selection
Warwickshire Railways

West Midlands

Bilston, Bradley &
  Ladymoor
Birmingham Transport
Black Country Pubs
Blackheath
Cradley Heath
Cradley Heath: A Second
  Selection
Darlaston, Moxley &
  Bentley
Great Bridge & District
Halesowen: A Second
  Selection
Ladywood
Ladywood Revisited
Lye & Wollescote
Lye & Wollescote: A Second
  Selection
Northfield Past & Present
Oldbury
Rowley
Sedgley: A Fourth Selection
Smethwick
Solihull
Stourbridge, Wollaston &
  Amblecote
Stourbridge, Wollaston &
  Amblecote: A Second
  Selection
Tipton: A Third Selection
Wednesbury
Wordsley

Wiltshire

Around Devizes
Around Highworth
Castle Combe to
  Malmesbury
Crewkerne & the Ham
  Stone Villages
Marlborough: A Second
  Selection
Salisbury: A Second
  Selection

Worcestershire

Worcester Past & Present

Yorkshire

Around Hoyland
Around Hoyland: A Second
  Selection
Doncaster
Huddersfield
Huddersfield: A Second
  Selection
Leeds in the News
Northallerton: A Second
  Selection
Pontefract
Sheffield
Shire Green, Wincobank &
  Ecclesfield
Wombwell & Darfield

Wales

Anglesey
Carmarthen & the Tywi
  Valley
Chepstow & The River
  Wye
Haverfordwest
Milford Haven
Upper Teifi
Welshpool

Scotland

Annandale
Around Lochaber
Clydesdale
Musselburgh
Perth
Selkirkshire
St Andrews

Ireland

Coleraine & the Causeway
  Coast